THE WAY UP CAME DOWN

THE WAY UP CAME DOWN

By Andrew Hronich

The Way Up Came Down

Trilogy Christian Publishers A Wholly Owned Subsidiary of Trinity Broadcasting Network

2442 Michelle Drive Tustin, CA 92780

For information about special discounts for bulk purchases, please contact Trilogy Christian Publishing.

Trilogy Disclaimer: The views and content expressed in this book are those of the author and may not necessarily reflect the views and doctrine of Trilogy Christian Publishing or the Trinity Broadcasting Network.

Manufactured in the United States of America

10 9 8 7 6 5 4 3 2 1

Library of Congress Cataloging-in-Publication Data is available.

ISBN: 978-1-64773-412-1

E-ISBN: 978-1-64773-413-8

To Andrew Daunarummo,
the man after whom I was named,
Thank you for inspiring me to keep writing, ever since I was a very young boy.
The hard work has finally paid off, in large part due to your encourage-
ment. You are the true patriarch of the family, a man who loves God and
puts Him first. You have helped me understand how incredibly minuscule
we are and how exceedingly immense He is.
For these reasons and more, I am eternally grateful.
Your loving grandson,
Drew

ACKNOWLEDGMENTS

To my parents, who from my youth have emulated the love of Christ in their discipline as well as through the innumerable ways they bless me.

To both extended and immediate family, such as my Aunt Ang and Uncle Rob, my siblings, and other close relatives who have watched me grow over the years and been present with me every step of the way.

To my brothers in Christ, such as Garison Allen, James Cummings, Garrett Dodson, Corey Hise, Jack Lipari, Ethan Mars, Lawrence McMath, Zane Mrazek, Evan Neil, Samuel Ortega, Alex and Dominic Turmene, and others, who continue to sharpen me with their keen insight and encourage me with their honest friendship.

To the pastors from my home church at Life Community Church in Jamestown, North Carolina: Pastors Jake Thornhill, Micah Ray, and Ryan Robertson, as well as Pastor Robert Murphey from Oakview Baptist Church, Dr. Allen McFarland from Liberty University, and my learned friend Chip Byrd.

Under the guidance of these titans of the faith, I have grown both as a leader and as a follower of Christ.

To my bosses, Matt Barber and Brad Self, along with my spiritual mentor, Brad Sterling, for the patient kindness they have shown to me. Words cannot express my gratitude towards each of them for showing me how a true man of God should act.

Finally, and most importantly, this book would be impossible but for the greatest Author of all, God Himself, to whom I owe all that I am and all that I have. Thank you, God, for giving me the ability to write this book. I sincerely desire that what I say is pleasing in your sight. I pray that your Word will echo in the pages of this book, and that lives will be transformed for your glory.

INTRODUCTION

Who am I? Why am I here? Questions of identity and purpose have plagued the human race from the moment breath entered our ancestors' lungs and thought patterns were conceptualized. Am I just another molecular substance in a vast universe, or is my identity found in something or someone beyond the limitations of this world?

In the modern era of TikTok and Coronavirus, human beings desperately attempt to maintain their grip on this world, but the statistics prove beyond a shadow of a doubt that every one of us is bound to walk through death's cruel doorpost. What lies beyond that doorway? Some say nothing. To some, life is summed up in the words of William Shakespeare: "It is a tale told by an idiot, full of sound and fury, signifying nothing" but to others, death is not a doorway to nothingness. It is the entrypoint to a new beginning.

Skeptics scoff at the seemingly inconceivable notion of a life following our present reality, and yet they are unable to answer why it is that eternity lies at the heart of every human being. We are all wired to desire life without end, but the question of how to secure this life remains a mystery to many. Where does that life take place and how do you get there?

Not surprisingly, different religions take different views. The Buddhists and Hindus believe in the concept of reincarnation, wherein we experience a repeated cycle of rebirth into different forms. Ultimately, our good works free us from this cycle, and the individual ceases to exist, having achieved the state of Nirvana, or nothingness. In contrast, Islam professes that after an individual's life on Earth, that individual will face judgment whereby he will either attain a life in Paradise or a life in Hell. According to the Koran, Allah alone, based on his own sovereign will, has the final say whether to affirm or deny an individual's entry into Paradise. Additionally, many other religions essentially say that if one's good works outweigh his bad works, he will earn his own way into some form of paradise.

Christianity provides a unique approach. Unlike with Buddhism and Hinduism, a person will never achieve a state of nothingness, but upon death will enter into either an eternal Heaven or Hell. Unlike with Islam, entrance into Heaven is not subject to a sovereign's unpredictable future judgment. Instead, the Bible contends that a person can be assured now of his future fate because humanity's entry price into Heaven costs nothing less than the precious blood of God Himself in the person of Jesus Christ. Thus, because Jesus has paid the entry price in full, all those who trust in His death, burial, and resurrection have the guarantee of life in Heaven. Additionally, this means that the Bible shuns the idea of human effort earning one a place in Heaven. When it comes time for them to face God, the Judge, He will see the life and death of Jesus

His Son (not their own deeds) and allow them safe passage into Heaven.

Initially, throughout the time of the Old Testament, God showed the way to Heaven by descending from on high, personally delivering His laws, and guiding His people in their ways. Ultimately, in the New Testament, the Way up came down in the person of Jesus Christ. Through Him, God invited humanity into a relationship with Him that surpassed even that of His seemingly perfect relationship with the first created human beings, Adam and Eve. Jesus, the self-described way to Heaven, demonstrated the way to relate to God on Earth and became the way to live with Him forever in Heaven. Accordingly, God adopted all those who trust in Jesus.

The Kingdom of Heaven is open to these redeemed sons and daughters of the King. But a person can be redeemed only if he or she knows the truth. This book does not teach new truth, rather it brings eternal truth into the light with the aim that orphans of Earth might become children of Heaven. For knowing that without Him we have no purpose and no future, the Way up came down.

CONTENTS

PART ONE

Detour: The Need for a Way

I: LIGHTNING THEN THUNDER

Date: Creation Past
Location: Heaven

A blinding streak of brilliant light blazed across the heavens. This was no mere meteor soaring through the immense darkness. Descending with greater speed and ferocity than a bolt of lightning, the streak was accompanied by a multitude of other streaks, all headed toward the same fate.

The streak was none other than the angel of light himself, Lucifer Morningstar (Is. 14:12), ruler of demons (Matt. 9:34), chief among the heavenly host (Ez. 28:14), and master of the heavenly choir (Ez. 28:13). He who once had risen above all other created beings had now fallen to a position lower than them all.

Lucifer, son of the dawn, had been reduced to a shadow of his former self (Is. 14:12). All around him, he could perceive the collateral damage of his ambitious yet futile grasp for power. Millions of angelic creatures, enthralled by Lucifer's words, attached their eternal destiny to his. So, when he was cast from Heaven, they were all cast down with him.

Even as he plummeted, Lucifer could still hear the archangel, Michael, and his fellow angels shouting, "Now the salvation and the power and the kingdom of our God and the authority of His Christ have come!" (Rev. 12:10). His lip curled in vehement distaste for the words of God's faithful, and his face contorted with disdain. They continued, "Therefore, rejoice O heavens and you who dwell in them! But woe to you, O earth and sea, for the devil has come down to you in great wrath, because he knows that his time is short!" (Rev. 12:12). Howling in rage, he clawed at his ears in vain effort to block the thunderous echo of the heavenly hosts resounding all around him:

Formerly, Lucifer had been an anointed cherub, a prominent brother in arms to Michael the mighty archangel. God had fashioned him and the other ministering angels from fire and had tasked them with executing His will (Heb. 1:7). He had been created pure and without blemish; yet, little by little, pride crept into his heart (Ez. 28:15). Instead of accepting his position and obeying God, he sought to establish himself on equal footing with Him. As a result, he rebelled against the King of Heaven and now suffered the horrific consequences.

The Syndrome Thesis

One cannot engage in a deep discussion about God without also acknowledging the existence of the devil. One of the hardest apologetical questions to answer is why did God create the devil? After all, God knew full well the evil he would bring.

My friends Wilmar and Jacob dubbed their answer to this dilemma the "Syndrome Hypothesis." In Pixar's *The Incredibles*, the antagonist, Syndrome, creates a deadly robot which kills superheroes and spreads mayhem, but which he alone can defeat. In his diabolical monologue, Syndrome, watching the lethal robot on the news, says, "The robot will emerge dramatically, do some damage, throw some screaming people, and just when all hope is lost, Syndrome will save the day! I'll be a bigger hero than [the Incredibles] ever were!" In short, Syndrome purposely creates a problem so that when he solves it, he will receive all the praise and credit.

For some people, this is how they view God's creation of Lucifer. To them, it seems that if God knows all things, and if He created all things, then He created Lucifer knowing that Lucifer would rebel. Thus, they argue that God purposely created Lucifer for the end goal of glorifying Himself.

While God might receive more glory following Lucifer's rebellion than He would have if Lucifer had never fallen, this does not by any means pin the blame squarely on God. Lucifer acted of his own free will, which God had granted him and all the angels. We can blame no one else but Lucifer for his own choices. God does not cause evil, but He can take that which was intended for evil and use it for good (Gen. 50:20; Rom. 8:28).

Eventually, had Lucifer not fallen, someone else likely would have, and then we would be posing to God the same question that we have concerning Lucifer. To make an analogy, many parents are willing to risk their children growing up to become sinful, immoral people, but this does not hinder their want for children. Nor would they force their children to obey them, even if they could. Instead, knowing that love requires a choice, they are willing to take the chance of their children disobeying and not loving them in return. Likewise, God, knowing the future sins of His Creation, still chose to create Satan and mankind out of His own desire and gave them a choice

Lucifer's Origin

While the purpose behind Satan's creation may be shrouded in mystery, the Bible does provide some insight regarding his initial origin. First, the devil, Lucifer, is a created being. God made him. As such, Lucifer and God are not equals. Using the king of Tyre as an allegorical reference to Lucifer, the Bible insinuates that he was a product of God's Creation: "Your settings and mountings were made of gold; on the day *you were created* they were prepared" (Ez. 28:13) (emphasis added). Thus, unlike what some posit, the universe does not exist in cosmic dualism where good and evil balance one another. Rather, God is the Almighty One on the throne, and Lucifer is merely one of His created subjects, whom God allows to rebel until His appointed time (Job 1:6).

Second, Lucifer was designed like all the other angels, blameless in the eyes of God. One theodicy (answer to the problem of evil) proposed by theologians is that God created a defective angel in the person of Lucifer; that is, that somehow God made a mistake. This line of belief contradicts not only what we know of God but also what is set forth in Scripture. God declares that Lucifer was "the seal of perfection, full of wisdom and beauty" (Ez. 28:12). He was numbered among the heavenly hosts with power and prestige to do God's work: "You were anointed as a guardian cherub, for so I ordained you" (Ez.

28:24). Lucifer's initial actions were holy and righteous: "You were blameless in your ways from the day you were created till wickedness was found in you" (Ez. 28:15). God did not slip up in crafting Lucifer substandard, instead Lucifer *chose* to rebel.

By all accounts, Lucifer initially pursued God's purpose and plan for Creation and could have been a chief instrument of God, a herald of God's wisdom to mankind, and an asset in humanity's early stages. Unfortunately, such was not the case. Little by little, Lucifer allowed evil to grab hold of his heart. What was the root of this evil?

The Ultimate Sin

As with human beings, the root of the evil began in Lucifer's heart. In a few short words, the Bible enlightens us concerning Lucifer's inner rebellion that preceded his external downfall: "Your heart became proud on account of your beauty, and you corrupted your wisdom because of your splendor. So, I threw you to the earth; I made a spectacle of you before kings" (Ez. 28:17). Day after day, Lucifer beheld the *shekinah* glory of God, glory beyond human comprehension, and upon observing it, and upon noticing his own splendor, Lucifer desired God's glory for himself. The wings which he had stretched out to shield himself from the magnificence of God's glory now reached out greedily to tear it from God. Thus, Lucifer began to devise mental blueprints of what life would look like if he were to reign in God's place.

The sad truth is that with all Lucifer's gifts, he chose to glorify the gift recipient instead of the Gift Giver. This self-focus led him to glory thieving. Are we not guilty of doing the same? We are quick to pass blame onto God when life disappoints us, but we prefer to gobble up glory when things go well. When we receive a job promotion or something for which we feel we have worked hard, too often we dismiss God's role in the blessing and appropriate the credit for ourselves. The reality is all our gains are due to God. As Jesus Himself noted, "[A]part from me you can do nothing" (John 15:5). Successes at work, in relationships, and in everyday life are all on account of Him.

Self-glorification is particularly prevalent throughout today's "I" generation, which is marked by not just "iPhones" and "iPads," but by "I think" and "I feel" and "I want." These are constant, dominating refrains that shape the way we live our lives. Through selfies, social media, and nearly everything we do, we seek to glorify ourselves. Not unlike Lucifer, we snatch at and steal God's fame for ourselves. This selfish lifestyle stems from one emotion and one characteristic: the sin of pride. Nearly every sin can be neatly tucked under the category of pride, whereby an individual focuses on himself vis á vis God and others.

Pride is the motivator, and covetousness is the deed. Pride plants the seed, and when full grown, sprouts covetousness, whereby people desire that which they do not have. This deadly combination eventually culminates in the demise of all those who remain steadfast in their sinful determination. Lucifer is no exception.

Lucifer's Endgame

As it often does, pride leads to other sins, and, in the case of Lucifer, it eventually leads to a desire to subvert the order of things. In this way, Lucifer mirrors the infamous Marvel villain, Thanos, who delivers a chilling speech towards the end of *Avengers: Endgame*. When countered by the staunch resistance of Captain America, Iron Man, and Thor, Thanos confesses his intentions to shred the universe down to its last atom and recreate all life according to his making. To put it in his words, "I'll create a new one, teeming with life, that knows not what it has lost, but only what it has been given. A grateful universe."

In response to Thanos' genocidal bloodlust, Captain America retorts, "Born out of blood."

With a wry grin spread across his face, Thanos answers him, "They'll never know it because you won't be alive to tell them."

Just as Thanos' ultimate plan was to wipe out the old order of things and institute a new one with no reminder of the past, Lucifer likewise hoped to accomplish a similar feat – with himself at the helm.

The prophet Isaiah offers insight into Lucifer's ambitions by relaying his rebellious inner thoughts.

> You said in your heart, "I will ascend to the heavens; I will raise my throne above the stars of God; I will sit enthroned on the mount of assembly, on the utmost heights of Mount Zaphon. I will ascend above the tops of the clouds; I will make myself like the Most High."
>
> Is. 14:13-14

A closer examination of Lucifer's internal desires reveals his multifaceted lust for power.

Lucifer's Gambit

First, notice that Lucifer purposed to ascend into the heavens. To ascend into the heavens was to abandon one's own position and to invade God's territory. In other words, he was planning a takeover.

This is very similar to an event a millennia later when the Roman general Gaius Julius crossed the Rubicon River. According to Roman law, upon the successful end to a military campaign, a Roman general was ordered to disband his army before crossing into his home province. In this manner, the Roman Republic hoped to avoid an imperium, whereby one man would employ the full force of the Roman army to establish himself as king of Rome. Julius intentionally defied this law by leading his army in the hopes of gaining absolute power. Julius is famously noted for having declared, before crossing over, "The die has been cast."

Likewise, when Lucifer says, "I will ascend above the tops of the clouds" (Is. 14:14), we see Lucifer's mock attempt at what Jesus Christ would later accomplish. After his resurrection, Jesus ascends above the clouds into Heaven by divine invitation (Acts 1). Lucifer, on the other hand, receives no such invitation. Rather, Lucifer's planned ascension reflects an intention of powerful conquest. Clearly, Lucifer wants to violate God's sovereign territory in a vain attempt at launching a coup. His goal is to possess more glory than God Himself. He does not simply want to become God's equal. He wants to become God's superior.

Ruler of Angels

Additionally, Lucifer's intentions after invading heaven were to rule over all the angels. He says, "I will raise my throne above the stars of God" (Is. 14:13). The Scriptures frequently use the term "stars" to refer to angels (Rev 1:20; 12:4). Lucifer clearly did not seek to bring about a democratic system whereby the angels would rule together as a united group with one voice. Instead, Lucifer hoped to reign supreme over all other angelic beings. Every angel would thus bow to him, and any who refused would suffer the same fate as Lucifer planned for God.

Ruler of Heaven

Furthermore, Lucifer was not invading Heaven to rule just the angels. Rather, he sought also to rule in God's stead. He claims, "I will sit enthroned on the mount of assembly, on the utmost heights of Mount Zaphon" (Is. 14:13). The "mount of assembly" often expressed ruling in God's kingdom (Is. 2:1-4). Here Lucifer reveals his desire to replace God. Moreover, what the New International Version translates as "Mount Zaphon," other Bible versions translate as "the north" (ESV; NASB; NKJV). "The north" often refers to God's presence (Ps. 75:6-7; 48:2) and it also refers to where Jesus will reign on the Earth in the last days. Thus, by saying that he will rule in "the north," Lucifer declares his intentions to supplant God and take His place at that time and forevermore.

Ruler of God

Last, Lucifer reveals his ultimate gal in Isaiah 14:14 – "I will make myself like the Most High."

El-Elyon, Most High God, is an epithet of God first used by Melchizedek, the priest and king of Salem, when addressing Abraham. The epithet refers to God's sovereignty over not only Earth, but Heaven as well. This same authority, the Father would later give Jesus (Matt. 28:18).

Seeking to usurp Jesus' inheritance, Lucifer planned to supplant God and take His place as the one true sovereign of the universe. This is the chief example of all his counterfeits, as all that he can offer are perverted substitutes. He presents us with false Christianity, a false Gospel (as Paul referred to it in Gal. 1:9), false gods (Ep. 2:2), false angels (2 Cor. 11:14), false apostles (2 Cor. 11:13), and false promises (Gen 3:5). He cannot create something out of nothing, like God can, so he exploits what God has already fashioned.

Thus, long before God created humanity in His image, Lucifer tried to counterfeit himself into God's image. He tried to steal what was God's alone to give away. This was the same temptation he would later extend to Eve, and the same temptation which plagues every human being. Each of us wants to be our own god, the ultimate authority in our life; but the problem is that God utterly and rightfully refuses to step aside. Thus, our attempts, as well as Lucifer's literal attempt, to become God are doomed to fail.

This reminds me yet again of a scene from Marvel's *Avengers: Infinity War* where the Mad Titan Thanos storms Thor's ship and massacres the Asgardians. After easily dispatching both superheroes Hulk and Thor, Thanos thwarts an assassination attempt by Loki. Yet, as Thanos dangles Loki in the air, his gauntlet closing around his windpipe, Loki groans, "You will never be a god!"

This scene in *Infinity War* epitomizes Lucifer's efforts. He went to extreme lengths, like Thanos did when he gathered the infinity stones, to usurp God's position. He strategized, gathered an army, and eventually launched an all-out assault. But no matter how hard he tried, his attempt at a power grab was in vain. He truly would never be a god.

Evil that Blinds Itself

Many people often wonder how Lucifer could be so absurd as to think that he could overthrow God. How could a finite being overpower the infinite? Although Lucifer, like all angels, beheld the unparalleled glory of God, he allowed his pride to blind him. Shrewd and overconfident, he foolishly convinced himself that in the long run, he could overpower God. So, giving scant thought to the potential consequences of his actions, he began plotting against God. Whether openly or in secret, we do not know. What we do know is that by the time Lucifer had propagated his campaign of lies and mistrust, a third of the heavenly host banded around him (Rev. 12:4). [1]

Lucifer and his followers overlooked the truth that there is and always will be only one God, and none beside Him. As sovereign Creator, His majesty and authority are unparalleled, and no matter how many angels or beings attempt to rip the scepter from His hand, no one can loosen His rightful grip. Driven by prideful aspirations, Lucifer and his followers were willing to risk everything they had in hopes that they might take what was not theirs. And, as the Bible reveals, Lucifer's pride would continue to infect not just angels but countless others.

War in Heaven

One of the greatest injustices ever done was to bring war to the holiest of places, the very abode of God. So determined was Lucifer for power that he disregarded the long-term consequences his war in Heaven might have. Thus, in a place epitomized for its peaceful conditions, Lucifer conducted the first battle.

The Bible gives very little clues as to what transpired in the course of Lucifer's struggle, but it likely was not a one-day event. The Book of Daniel references spiritual warfare when an angel attempted to visit the prophet Daniel and was prevented by demonic forces for twenty-one days before the archangel Michael came to help him (Dan. 10:13). If demonic forces were able to prevent an angelic messenger from bringing God's Word to His servant for twenty-one days, I can only imagine how long Lucifer strove in Heaven to overthrow God and His angels.

Interestingly, when the battle is described in Revelation 12, nowhere is God's direct activity attributed. Instead, God's representative in the form of Michael the archangel leads the other angels against Lucifer and his demons (Rev. 12:7). Despite all his schemes and his prowess, Lucifer was unable to reach the "big boss." Instead, his attempts were thwarted by one of God's servants as a means of humbling Lucifer. In this manner, God revealed how greatly Lucifer overestimated his abilities. He thought he could challenge God, but he could not even overcome another angel. Revelation 12:8 perfectly sums up Lucifer's attempt: "But he was not strong enough, and they lost their place in heaven."

The demons bet everything they had on Lucifer, but in the hour when they needed him most, Lucifer failed. This was his moment, his time to establish his rule. But before his very eyes, he watched his plan crumble into ruins. Thus, Lucifer and his followers were forcefully hurled to the Earth, having forfeited their place in Heaven.

Barred from Heaven

Hell was not Lucifer's home. He and all his followers were created "in" and "for" Heaven. Thus, when they were cast from Heaven, they were cast from their home. Never would Lucifer forget the joy of Heaven, and whenever he would recall such things, he would gnash his teeth. Such memories brought only pain and hatred of former things to himself.

To Lucifer's surprise, God did not simply consign him and his demons to oblivion. Rather, God allotted Lucifer and his rebels a place in Hell, prepared especially for Lucifer and those like him. Terrified, Lucifer wondered when the judgment day might come, but God made it clear that only He knew the day and that Lucifer would forever tread on his tippy toes, not knowing when the hour would arrive.

Unable, as all angels are, to repent of his sin, Lucifer conspired further against God. He refused to wait out his years in misery. Rather, if God had already sentenced him to a life of eternal torment, why not live out the rest of his years opposed to God and His plan? Thus, Lucifer turned his eyes towards the gem of God's Creation, hoping that by some guile he might cause God's prize to suffer the same fate as his.

Conclusion

Eastern religions such as Daoism embrace the concept of cosmic dualism, whereby good and evil exist in a delicate balance. However, the Bible does not support the co-eternality of good versus evil. Rather, God, who is perfect and holy, created everything in a pure, harmonic state. Evil did not exist in God's perfect world, but all created beings had a choice whether to serve God or themselves. Satan was the first rebel.

While culture embraces rebels as heroes and freedom fighters, rebellion is seated in the narcissistic actions of Lucifer and his rebels. They sought to uproot God and His universal system of law, but God proved once and for all that He reigns unchallenged and unmatched. Thus, from the moment of his fall, Lucifer's name was changed to that of HaSatan (Satan), the adversary, who would forever be a thorn in the flesh to all of God's Creation. May we, through the power of the Spirit, resist his lies and all his counterfeit paths.

II: GPS (GOD'S PERFECT STORY)

Date: Beginning of Time
Location: Garden of Eden

The cool breeze gently greeted the Garden of Eden as the birds chirped joyously, welcoming the fresh dawn of morning. Everything was yet young and innocent among all Creation, for in six days, God had created, out of nothing, the vast universe and everything therein. Even so, God discerned that there was something missing, something special He had not yet formed.

Reaching out His hand, God clutched a fistful of dust in His palm and held it up for inspection. The closer He brought the dust to His face, the louder He heard the sounds of laughter and shouts of praise. God discerned the countless descendants, full of life and happiness, who would follow from this very plot of dust. But in that same moment, God also heard horrible wailing and frightful screams. Anger flared and explosions echoed in His ears, as God deciphered the strife and sin that would arise on account of mankind's choices.

Weighing the dust in His hand, God hesitated. If He were to create mankind, He would enable the created order to fall into chaos, to suffer unwantedly for man's actions. Yet, God did not cast the dust aside. Rather, He tenderly folded His fingers around the handful of dirt and crafted the jewel of His Creation. From His mouth issued galaxies, and yet the product of His fingers far surpassed even the luster of the celestial stars. Thus, on the sixth day, God formed man.

Nevertheless, the man was only a shell. It needed more than just God's touch. It required the very presence of God exhibited through His Spirit. For this purpose, the Spirit of God imbued the man with His lifegiving, life-sustaining power. Infused with God's own breath of life, man became a living being! Designed with purpose, the man praised Creator God for the unparalleled, unspeakable gift of life.

The A-Z God

From the very first sentence in Genesis, the Bible irrefutably identifies the protagonist of the Scriptures. "In the beginning, *God* created the heavens and the earth" (Gen. 1:1) (emphasis added). The Bible does not begin by centering on man and his achievements in the Garden. Rather, from the outset, the Bible makes it perfectly clear that everything, every event, and every person exists *because* of God and *for* God. He is not a supporting character in our story, rather, He is the central figure, and we live in His story.

So, who is God? And where did He come from?

When the prophet Moses wrote the book of Genesis, he cleverly crafted the first verse of Genesis through the use of seven words (seven being the Hebrew number for completeness). However, the English translations often omit one Hebrew word, for it is not a word at all. Located between the phrases "In the beginning" and "God." Moses wrote a qualifier to describe God. This qualifier was composed of the first and last Hebrew letters (*tav* and *alef*) so that in our language, it would have read something like "AZ." Why did Moses do so? Because He was identifying the God of Creation as the eternal, omniscient One who existed before time, space, or matter, and who transcends all created things.

"I am the first and I am the last; apart from me there is no God" (Is. 44:6). There is not a pantheon of gods, like the Greeks, Romans, and other ancient civilizations believed. Rather, there is one God, and He is the Creator of all that the eye can and cannot see. To the Gentiles, He is the alpha and omega, and to the Jews, He is the tav and alef, He who was and is and is to come (Rev. 1:8).

The Creator God

Fascinatingly, the very first action the Bible ascribes to God is of creating. What did God create? Genesis 1:1 says, "In the beginning, God created *the heavens and the earth.*" (emphasis added). Nothing in the entire universe found its source independent of the Creator. "For in him all things were created: things in heaven and on earth, visible and invisible, whether thrones or powers or rulers or authorities; all things have been created through him and for him" (Col. 1:16).

From galaxies to mountains to oceans to the complex components of air, God made it all. Every animal and every plant, He crafted it and sanctified it. Often overlooking the brilliance of His unfathomable wisdom, we choose to elevate the knowledge of men and praise "geniuses" such as Albert Einstein and Sir Isaac Newton. But God is the one who created the material which these men studied – and even created the mental capabilities of the men themselves! He is the genius of geniuses, having fashioned the gigantic universe even down to the complex microscopic cell for His pleasure.

Of all Creation, God placed at the forefront Heaven and Earth. During Creation Past, an unspecified period that occurred before the seven days of Creation in Genesis 1, God created Heaven itself (Gen. 1:1). This was to be His abode. While many people consider Heaven to be nothing more than a metaphor, Scripture makes it abundantly clear that Heaven is a substantive location created by God in another dimension. It is here that God chooses to reside in unapproachable light (1 Tim. 6:16). Even so, He does not reside in Heaven alone. Rather, God displays His relational side by creating the heavenly host consisting of angelic beings formed for the sole purpose of ministering to God and His Creation. Day and night, the host of Heaven sings praises to God, their Creator and King, acknowledging His glory in the highest (Rev. 7:15).

Second to Heaven alone in its splendor, God created a second Paradise, Earth. Conditions on Earth are perfect for life, with no other planet in the universe being capable of supporting sentient life. For one thing, Earth's atmosphere is composed of 21% oxygen. If the atmosphere was made of 25% oxygen, the earth would dissolve in flames. If only 15%, we would suffocate. Just as God infused oxygen in the lungs of the first human being, so He infused Earth's atmosphere with the perfect balance of gases. The transparency of the Earth's atmosphere, the tilt of the Earth's axis, the shape of

Earth's elliptical orbit, and the speed of Earth's rotation are all marks of perfection. Had any designer other than God attempted to fashion the Earth, it would have been impossible, but God created the planet absolutely perfect, with no room for improvement.

Order Out of Chaos

Curiously, while Genesis 1:1 records the creation of the heavens and the earth, Genesis 1:2 says that "the earth was void and without form." How can this be if the prophet Isaiah says that God does not make anything without form (Is. 45:18)?

The Hebrew word for without form (wa-bohu) means wasteland, or that which is laid to waste, while the Hebrew word for void (tohu) refers to an undistinguishable ruin. Who or what is responsible for this ruin? Surely not God, for why would He create something only to devastate it?

Recall that when God banished Lucifer from Heaven, the angels cried out, "Woe to the earth and the sea, because the devil has gone down to you! He is filled with fury, because he knows that his time is short" (Rev. 12:2). The devil was not cast to Hell, but rather, he fell to the earth and sea, and in his wrath, he sought to dismantle God's Creation. As a murderer, he sought to kill Creation; as a thief, he sought to rob God's joy and purpose; and as a destroyer, he sought to mare God's perfect story.

In Psalm 104, King David provides a retelling of Creation and records that following God's creation of the seas, "the waters stood above the mountains" (Ps. 104:6). Satan could not prevent God from creating, but perhaps he could mare God's Creation to the point that God would desist from His purpose. Nevertheless, God refused to be thwarted. "But at your rebuke the waters fled, at the sound of your thunder they took to flight; they flowed over the mountains, they went down into the valleys, to the place you assigned for them" (Ps. 104:7-8).

God had made up His mind long before Satan ever existed that He would create a universe of His liking, and no demon or angel could thwart Him. With a strong rebuke, He commanded the waters to desist, and when the waters subsided, what remained was His purpose, established from eternity and manifest in the present age.

The Creation of Mankind

God did not stop His Creation at Heaven. He may have started with what the angels imagined having been the pinnacle of the created order, but throughout the seven days of Creation, He progressively moved towards the greatest creation of all: mankind.

While during the other six days of Creation God spoke the created order into being, He did not do so with humanity. Humanity was unique.

With full agreement within the Trinity, God said, "Let *us* make mankind in *our* image, in *our* likeness, so that they may rule over the fish in the sea and the birds in the sky, over the livestock and all the wild animals, and over all the creatures that move along the ground" (Gen. 1:26) (emphasis added). The Father orchestrated the design, the Son created the man, and the Spirit breathed into the man the gift of life.[2] The first human being exemplified the union of flesh and spirit, of Heaven and Earth. God had indeed saved the best for last, which was why after creating mankind, "God *blessed* them and said to them, 'Be fruitful and increase in number; fill the earth and subdue it. Rule over the fish in the sea and the birds in the sky and over every living creature that moves on the ground'" (Gen. 1:28) (emphasis added). Genesis does not record God bestowing such a blessing on any other part of Creation, for mankind was set apart as the crown jewel of God's Creation.

What made mankind so important to God? Sadly, some false teachers today claim that Jesus suffered and died for us because we are worthy of the love of God. This unsubstantiated, anthropocentric claim undermines not only the wonder of Jesus' redemption but also the mystery of Creation. Nothing God created could ever be worthy of His love, for to be so, the created object would need to be equal to God Himself. God has no equal. Even in a perfect, wondrous state, mankind was still unworthy of the love of God. God did not make humanity worthy of His love, but rather, He chose to love us despite our unworthiness. God does not love us because we are valuable. Rather, we are valuable because God loves us.

Imago Dei

In Genesis 1, when Moses records the creation of man, he places this event after God commands for all living things to produce according to their kind. Thus, all land and sea animals produce according to their kind, and it is only after God issues this command that He makes man in a way after His kind, that is, in His image and His likeness. Thus, mankind acts as a reflection (not a reproduction) of God Himself, a gift not granted to even the host of heaven. Humanity alone was to bear this greatest gift of God, His very own image (Gen. 1:26).

Interestingly, one of the greatest offenses against God is that of ascribing an image to God (Ex. 20:4). Yet Genesis 1:27 scandalously states that God created mankind in His image. How do these two truths coincide?

When human beings attempt to make God into an image, they attempt to bind the limitless God. They are not necessarily trying to create a new god, but rather they are attempting to constrain the glory of God to an object of Creation. In their finite nature, human beings simply cannot construct an image capable of accomplishing that feat.

Conversely, God declares human beings to be His image bearers. This is possible since, unlike human beings, God has both the authority and ability to construct a vessel He deems suitable. That chosen vessel is mankind.

But what does it mean to bear the image of God? The image of God refers to several key qualities human beings possess that are unique to God and people. Animals and angels do not share all these qualities.

First, the image of God refers to the substantive nature of humanity. The substantive nature of humanity refers to the intellectual, emotional, and volitional characteristics of humanity. Humanity possesses both spirit and body, and in this capacity, people are able to develop personality and utilize their free will.

Second, human beings are relational, as God is relational. As Adam and Eve, the first man and woman, became one flesh, so God Himself is three-in-one. In this relational capacity, mankind is better able to understand and reflect the divine nature of God.

Lastly, the image of God is reflected in the functional nature of mankind. God gave humanity the creation mandate so that mankind might subdue the earth for their pleasure (Gen. 1:28). In their roles as sovereigns of Creation, human beings reflect their Creator, who Himself is sovereign. Yet, not only do human beings rule Creation, but they also care for it, as Adam and Eve maintained the Garden of Eden at God's behest. In this manner, they mirror God, who not only created the heavens and the earth, but who also maintains them by His divine power. Furthermore, human beings are gifted with the ability to procreate, giving life to others just as God gave life to them.

In all these ways, people reflect the unique nature of God. Just imagine -- every human being from every tribe, nation, race, and ethnicity on the face of the earth has been made in the image of the Almighty God. What a priceless gift that God has chosen to weave His own image into the very fabric of our being, infusing us with immeasurable worth.

Innate Value

The existence of God as Creator provides humanity with value and purpose. If there were no creator, and mankind existed simply due to mere luck, people would have no innate value. Sure, humanity could ascribe worth and purpose to itself, but the basis for that would necessarily be subjective. The existence of God as Creator, however, dictates that our value and purpose are intrinsically given by Him and not manufactured, or variable based on our changing feelings or philosophies.

We are not biological, molecular structures wandering aimlessly with no end goal, but rather we are purposefully created beings, specifically designed by the Maker's hand. Our value does not come from the worth we or even others assign to us, but instead our worth derives from the very One who fashioned us from the beginning. What the world may declare worthless, God gazes upon as His beloved creation. No matter where we live, what we look like, what we own, what we have done – because of Him, our lives have meaning.

From Dust

At the same time, it is important to remember that God formed man from the dust of the earth. Man was created last after all the animals and all the vastness of God's Creation, and as such, his role is that of a subordinative, nurturing role. God could have crafted man from gold or silver, but instead, He illustrated to the first man and all his descendants the ultimate value of man apart from God. Without God, man is but dust, blown hither and thither by the wind, but God's power and benevolence is able to craft a treasure from the most worthless object.

Therefore, a careful balance must be ascribed when measuring the worth of humanity. Without the breath of God, we are worthless and lifeless; but with the breath of God in us, our value outweighs even that of the stars in the sky!

Not Good

Up until this point, everything God created He declared to be good, but upon perceiving the man's loneliness, God sympathized for Adam's plight. At this point, God declared, "It is not good for man to be alone" (Gen. 2:18). Human beings are relational beings, and, as such, they are not meant for isolation.

At first, God brought all the animals before Adam, but even the dogs were not suitable companions. Man was different from the rest. A longing lingered in his heart, a longing that could be fulfilled only by a relationship with one in his likeness. For this end, God performed the first surgical procedure, putting the man asleep and forming a being in Adam's likeness from the man's rib.

Guiding the new created being, God brought her to the man. Upon beholding a being in his likeness, Adam marveled. "She shall be called Woman," he said, "for she was taken out of Man." Thus, Adam realized that there can be male, only if there is also female. Woman only if there is also man. Man and woman were created to aid one another in serving God. Fashioned from man's side, woman stands beside man as his partner. And joined together, they become one flesh.

Divine Law

As the adage goes, "Freedom isn't free." Even in a perfect environment such as Eden, God mandates certain laws for mankind to abide by. First and foremost, God commands Adam, "You are free to eat from any tree in the garden; but you must not eat from the tree of the knowledge of good and evil, for when you eat from it you will certainly die" (Gen. 2:16-17).

God makes the terms of His relationship with humanity clear from the outset. Compliance will lead to blessing; disobedience shall lead to both spiritual and physical death. This is not a relationship of equals, rather, Adam and Eve must satisfy the condition of obedience to maintain a relationship with God. God's divine laws cannot be altered, but they can be obeyed or disobeyed. For the time being, Adam decides to obey, and peace and prosperity exist on the earth.

Conclusion

From the beginning, the relational, sovereign God made Himself known by creating the world. John Calvin, in *The Sermon of All Creation: Christians on Nature*, remarked, "The Creation is quite like a spacious and splendid house, provided and filled with the most exquisite, and at the same time, the most abundant furnishings. Everything in it tells of God." All Creation reveals God's glory, but none as much as mankind, who was made in God's own image. Amazingly, God descended from Heaven, stooped to the ground, and formed the prize of Creation from the dust. Heaven's breath filled Earth's lungs. The "Way Up" came down and gave humanity the breath of His life.

III: IT'S TO DIE FOR

Date: Earth's Early Years
Location: Garden of Eden

Crawling on his feet, head held high, a mysterious serpent steadily crept through the lush undergrowth in the Garden. This odd creature was familiar with the variety of delicacies surrounding him. But today he had a grander plan than selecting which plant was on the breakfast menu. Today his actions were much more sinister, and they were not his own. Satan, utilizing his demonic powers of possession, controlled the serpent's every move.

Ever since God had exiled him from Heaven, Satan had desired revenge. His wicked spirit howled in anger and disgust upon beholding the tranquility of the Garden. How he craved to descend on the Earth and subdue it at the point of the sword, but God obstructed Satan's malicious schemes. Yet, after much persistent prompting, God provided Satan explicit permission to enter the Garden and test Adam and Eve. Satan might not be able to overtake humanity with a sword, but he would confront them with a forked tongue. Thus, with devious intentions, Satan entered the Garden in search of God's two stewards, and he did so in the guise of a serpent.

The Serpent

On the sixth day of Creation, God made all the land-dwelling animals, including the serpent, a reptile in the snake family. The serpent in the Garden was likely not a miniature garden snake, as many have envisioned. Rather, it probably was a monstrous creature of gigantic proportions. This enormous, malicious, Satan-possessed serpent has spurred imitations in various ancient cultures. The Norse believed in a colossal Midgard serpent, capable of enwrapping the globe, which would one day bring about Ragnarök, the world's end. The Egyptians feared Apophis, the gargantuan demonic serpent that threatened to plunge the world into chaos. The Ancient Near Eastern culture wrote creational tales surrounding Tiamat and Lotan, giant serpents that waged war against the celestial gods. The Jews feared the Leviathan, a ferocious, scaly, sea serpent capable of exuding bursts of flames. All these stories have a common thread running through them: they all point to a monstrous, fearsome serpent bent on wreaking turmoil in the world. All these myths and legends stem from the Biblical account in which Satan entered into the serpent, a majestic beast, to return the world to a chaotic state.

Why then do most Christians imagine the serpent as diminutive in nature? Perhaps it is a misunderstanding perpetuated by Satan himself to minimize his perceived role in humanity's fall. While Satan needed to command Eve's attention in the Garden, having achieved his goal he now chooses to operate undetected. What better way to make his presence seem near innocuous than to have us conceive of the Garden serpent as a tiny garden snake? In so doing we can more readily blame Adam and Eve or even God Himself and overlook Satan's deception. This way, Satan can subtly remove himself from the picture.

The Father of Lies

Satan was purposeful in possessing a serpent to approach Eve, for "the serpent was more crafty than any of the wild animals the Lord God had made" (Gen. 3:1).

Sometimes, we like to think of ourselves as crafty. We fancy that we can figure our way around things or even outsmart members of the spiritual realm, but we are fooling ourselves if we think we can outwit the devil. Cunning is his figurative middle name; deceiver is his first. He is smarter and more clever than any of us. Nonetheless, we do have a way to avoid succumbing to his temptations: we can overpower him in the Name of Jesus, who has given us "authority to trample on snakes and scorpions and to overcome all the power of the enemy" (Luke 10:19).

We must remain alert, though, because Satan does not approach us with obvious evil intent, but rather, he comes to us in disguise. Regarding Satan's character, Jesus Himself proclaimed, "He was a murderer from the beginning, not holding to the truth, for there is no truth in him. When he lies, he speaks his native language, for he is a liar and the father of lies" (John 8:44). Masquerading himself as an angel of light, he spins his webs of lies and deceit in hopes of ensnaring as many people as possible. Indeed, if we imagine him as popular culture depicts him (a harmless red-skinned figure with a forked tail, pair of horns, and a pitchfork), we will not take him seriously and will thereby render ourselves vulnerable to his schemes.

He had deceived the angels of Heaven, and now, he had turned his sights on the guardians of Earth. How would they respond to his lies? Would they fall like the countless angels who sided with him, or would they hold fast to God's Word?

The Absence of Relationship

So, what happened after Satan came creeping up to Eve? Genesis declares: "[The serpent] said to the woman, 'Did God really say, "You must not eat from any tree in the garden"?'" (Gen. 3:1).

First, notice Satan's insight. How did Satan know of God's command? Did God tell him? Did he overhear Adam talking with Eve? While we might not know exactly how Satan discovered God's command for Adam and Eve not to eat of the fruit, we do know Satan did his research. Whether or not we realize it, Satan and his minions stalk all of us daily. Just as online companies use cookies to track our behavior and habits to learn what advertisements to show us, Satan and his demons carefully study us to identify how best to entice us to sin. We must be vigilant, therefore, to recognize their tactics and our own temptations.

Additionally, notice that Satan did not mind talking about God. The very first recorded conversation in the Bible between two created beings concerned the person of God. Yet, Satan threw a curveball, as should be expected of him, but one which Eve did not catch.

Upon the creation of man, every time the Creator was referenced, He was referred to as the "Lord God." The "Lord" referred to God's covenant relationship with His people. Whenever Satan mentioned the Creator in Genesis 3, however, he referred to the Creator only as "God." This was no coincidence. Satan purposely left out this covenantal aspect of God's name, for Satan does not mind us talking about God, so long as we leave the relationship aspect out of the picture. We can mention His name all we desire. If we lack a personal relationship with Him, Satan has nothing to fear.

Moreover, "Lord" referred to God's sovereignty, and if there was anything Satan hated, it was the sovereignty of God. Of all God's Creation, Satan understood God's sovereignty the most, having faced utter humiliation on account of his failed coup. Thus, Satan sought to deconstruct God's sovereignty in Eve's eyes.

The Danger of Questions

Beware of statements posed as questions. Often, hidden agendas are insinuated in seemingly harmless questions. The query Satan posed to Eve was no exception. Prior to his confrontation with Eve, the Bible recorded no questions. There were only answers. Thus, the first recorded question was a manipulative tool of Satan.

So what was Satan's hidden agenda? To entice Eve to question God's Word and to insinuate that she had the authority to do so. John MacArthur, in Part 1 of his sermon series *The Fall of Man*, put it this way: "The most deadly force ever released into the world...is the assumption that what God said is subject to our judgment." Indeed, he proffered, "All temptation starts with the idea that we have a right to evaluate what God said or required." In fact, once we believe we can be critical of and not subject to God's Word, we become susceptible to unlimited deception.

Before Satan's suggestion, no human being had ever questioned God's motives or His Word. This is a far cry from today where the world has become so corrupted by sin that not a moment transpires where men do not scrutinize God's motives or doubt His Word. The devil was shrewd. His question was a mere pretense intent on drawing Eve to a conclusion he had already predesigned. He had only to lead Eve there.

Why Eve?

So, why did the devil single out Eve? Why not first attempt to seduce Adam? Many theologians propose the possibility that Satan knew the woman to be a weaker vessel (1 Pet. 3:7), but Scripture does not fully support this hypothesis. The Bible does confirm that only Eve was deceived by the serpent's wiles (1 Tim. 2:14). However, notice that it took six verses before Eve fell (Gen. 3:1-6), while Adam was convinced in the length of half a verse (Gen. 3:6). Eve actually proved harder to overcome than Adam, so this probably was not the reason why Satan singled her out. Perhaps his purpose was far more sinister, even biological.

Recall that angels do not have the ability to procreate. The number of the starry host will never waver, neither increasing nor decreasing. Human beings, however, can procreate, giving life to countless descendants. Satan knew this, having perceived God's command for humanity to be fruitful and multiply (Gen. 1:28). Thus, Satan utilized this knowledge for his own purposes.

If he could seduce Eve, the mother of all the living, he could obtain an army of followers. He was not attempting to seduce humanity merely to have them smitten by God and to derail God's relationship with them. Rather, he was still scheming how he might overthrow the Almighty. Perhaps human beings were the key. Maybe, if he could manipulate Eve, her descendants would swarm to his banner. To achieve this goal, Satan must recruit Eve, who would be the key to his future success.

Yet, should his plan go awry and if God chose to smite Adam and Eve, then Satan reasoned that God's punishment of mankind would fill Hell with as many image bearers of God as possible. Perhaps Lucifer does this believing that in some sense this would fill Hell with a piece of God. Or perhaps he desires to recreate man in his own image. Either way, a perpetual liar and deceiver, Lucifer distorts the way up so that we would become eternally lost.

Run from Sin

Interestingly, when Satan meets Eve, we do not know for sure where they are. We do know that they eventually wind up at the Tree of the Knowledge of Good and Evil, that is, the very tree with the forbidden fruit. And we do know that when Eve responds to Satan, she could clearly view the tree, as the Bible says that she "saw" the fruit of the tree (Gen. 3:6).

There are times when we think that we are driving our desires towards the destination we choose. Before we know it, though, sin has grabbed hold of the steering wheel and is directing us towards its devious end. In the words of theologian Ravi Zacharias, "Sin will take you farther than you want to go, keep you longer than you want to stay, and cost you more than you want to pay." Thus, knowing the nature and progression of sin, we should seek to stay as far away from it as possible, not linger anywhere near it. For, as we edge ever closer toward the chasm of sin, it takes only one slip and we tumble over the precipice.

While Eve's one mistake was being within the reach of sin, her other mistake was conversing with the devil. God tells us to flee from evil, not to consult it (1 Cor. 10:13). We are to rebuke Satan in the name of the Lord, not to give him an audience, lest we become tempted and then sin. Notably, Eve does not even question the fact that the serpent can talk. She just carries on a normal conversation as if this were an everyday thing. This is not the *Chronicles of Narnia*. Nowhere in Scripture, other than the account of Balaam and his donkey, do we see reference to talking animals. Yet, instead of running from the talking serpent, instead of questioning him, she begins to question God. She begins listening to the wrong voice.

Can the same be said of us today? Do we, like Eve, reject God's Word and lend an ear to the wrong voice? Finding a voice that will agree with our discontent takes little effort, and, ironically enough, when we find that voice, we tend not to question it. Why do we have no qualms with doubting God's voice but do not even bother to question Satan's? Instead, we should vigilantly check all voices against the Truth of God's Word. In the words of Scripture, "Resist the devil, and he will flee from you" (James 4:7). Give in to him, and he will destroy you.

Questioning the Word of God

"Did God really say, 'You must not eat from any tree in the garden'?" (Gen. 3:1). Satan's prime strategy that he employs in the Garden and in the rest of Scripture is to call into question the Word of God. When Satan asks Eve, "Did God really say," he is calling into question God's command that He gave to Adam and Eve not to eat of the forbidden fruit. Satan thereby reduces God's command to a question. Whenever he succeeds, he lessens the impact of God's Word.

Satan pulls this same trick on us today, convincing us to doubt a whole host of God's commands:

"Can you really believe the Bible? It was written so long ago, and it's been translated so many times that whatever we have today is not even close to the original."

"Did God really say not to…? Doesn't He want you to be happy?"

"Won't He forgive you anyway?"

Satan's strategy is a double-edged sword. He means both to cause us to doubt the imperative nature of God's commands as well as to view them as limiting or absurd. "Did God *really* say we should not commit adultery? Maybe He just meant that for people who were happily married." Or, "How could He expect us to stay faithful to just one person for our whole lives? That's impossible." Similarly, "If He really loved us, why would He want me to be unhappy?" In essence, Satan seeks to reduce God's command to a question and thereby lessen the authority of the command and allow it to be scrutinized by our judgment. But God's Throne is His own. His commands are not for human beings or angels to judge. Rather, they are for all Creation to obey.

So, when the serpent whispers in your ear that the Bible cannot be trusted or that it is absurd, tell him, "Let God be true, and every human being a liar!" (Rom. 3:4).

Do Not Add Unto God's Word

"We may eat of the fruit of the trees in the garden," Eve confirms, "but God said, 'You shall not eat of the fruit of the tree that is in the middle of the garden, neither shall you touch it, lest you die'" (Gen. 3:3). In Eve's defense of God's command, she committed a fatal flaw by ascribing words to God that He never said. He never told her that if she touched the tree, she would perish.

God unequivocally cautions us about changing His Word: "Do not add to what I command you and do not subtract from it, but keep the commands of the LORD your God that I give you" (Deut. 4:2). He was not joking.

What Eve did, even if well-meaning, was take the Lord's Name in vain. By attributing words to God that He did not say, like Eve, we too expose our faith to corruption. We endanger undermining our faith in the true Word of God. If Satan can damage our notions of what we believe God said, then he can cause us to doubt what God actually, genuinely affirmed.

Questioning the Character of God

Satan's next move was to question the character of God. Now that he has tried to sow doubt about God's message, he will attack the very basis of God's command by calling into question God's character.

"You will not certainly die," the serpent said to the woman, "For God knows that when you eat from it your eyes will be opened, and you will be like God, knowing good and evil" (Gen.

3:4-5). Satan began with a question, and now, he ends with a statement. That is how he operates. He starts off by planting doubt, and then he offers his solution to the very dilemma he has created! What was at first a question is now a blatant lie. What is worse, Satan, the father of lies, calls God a liar!

Moreover, Satan wants Eve to believe that there are no consequences for her sin, no final judgment. Many "Christian" cults today teach this heretical lie that because of God's endless love, He will not punish sinners for their misdeeds. However, they totally overlook another attribute of God: His justice. God makes it abundantly clear throughout the Scriptures that there will be a day on which every human being will be called to give an account for his or her life. Just as there are consequences for our decisions in this world, so there will be eternal consequences in the next.

In his temptation of Eve, Satan wanted Eve to forget the consequences of sin and to focus on the reward. He was not ignorant. He knew that when we recall the consequences of sin, we are more likely on the whole to forsake our fleshly desires, knowing that temporary pleasures do not compare with eternal consequences.

Thus, it is important to note that Eve's sin was not limited to eating the fruit. Before that, she sinned when she stopped believing in God's goodness and started thinking to herself, "Surely, a good God would not punish His own creation. Surely, He did not mean to restrict humanity from living life to the fullest." Whenever we doubt God's goodness, we, like Eve, plummet down a slippery slope, which leads to nothing but greater wickedness.

Like God

Additionally, in his proposal, Satan insinuates that God, for jealous reasons, is holding out on Adam and Eve. He implies that God is restraining them from greater freedom.

Satan convinces many people of this same lie today. He tries to tell single people that God is keeping them from the freedom of sex, when, in reality, God is protecting them from the detrimental consequences of extramarital intimacy. Rather than emphasize the true liberation provided by the bounds of God's love, Satan emphasizes the one item that God retains.

We become like the child on Christmas who receives many gifts, and yet, when he does not get the one gift he wanted, he complains. Instead of enjoying all the many other gifts he was generously showered with, he chooses to focus on the one thing "withheld" from him.

Coupled with this lie is the promise of divine status. Satan promises Eve a new nature, should she eat the fruit. No longer will she be submissive. Rather, she will be like God. This is the quintessential lie of the devil, that human beings can replace God in authority and knowledge. Both are interconnected. Satan tells Eve that she shall have the knowledge of good and evil, apart from God's Word. Her experiences will dictate her understanding.

Often in today's world, we are told to trust our feelings. One of the most famous lines in the *Star Wars* saga is "Search your feelings!" Untold films similarly advocate, "Follow your heart!" But God never tells us to rely solely on experiential knowledge or feelings. On the contrary, He warns us that "[t]he heart is deceitful above all things" (Jer 17:9).

God alone provides eternal, unchanging truth, given from the only One capable of discerning it from beginning to end. Yet, with the acquisition of knowledge, human beings feel compelled to tell God what He should and should not do. Satan insinuates that with knowledge comes power, promising Eve that should she gain this knowledge, her nature will be changed, and she will become like God. Her motives for wanting to be like God are irrelevant, whether because she admired Him and wanted to imitate Him or because she deviously hoped to usurp His authority. The reason is because, either way, she still sought to achieve god-status and supplant Him as the sole cosmic sovereign. But God is a jealous God.

Jealous God

If there is anything that God cannot stand it is someone else attempting to usurp His place. "That's egotistical," some argue; but put yourself in God's shoes. Paul Washer uses this analogy in the film *American Gospel*. Imagine that you built your billion-dollar company from scratch and that you are sitting in your office one day when some guy from off the streets comes storming in and tells you he is taking over. He then starts to give orders to your employees, take funds, and use them as he saw fit, even though he played no part in the company you built. Indignant, you would storm out of your office bellowing, "Who do you think you are? This is not your company!"

Washer explained it this way:

You would be rightfully jealous for the thing that you had created. Would you reserve the right for you to feel that way, for you to burn with righteous jealousy over the things that you created, and yet you say that God has no right to be jealous over the things He has made? He has every right. This is His world.

Aside from God having all rights to establish the rules for the world that He has made, He is also the only one capable of properly executing that role. He is all-knowing, all-powerful, omnipresent, and eternal. Imagine us thinking *we* are more qualified to make the rules! Accepting that there is a God and we are not Him provides a more clear perspective. Unfortunately, most people choose to either doubt the existence of God, or they elevate themselves to God's status. My grandfather said it best when I was young. "You're a passenger in life. Do not try to replace God in the driver seat. If you do, you'll only drive that car farther away from the blessed destination God intends for you."

Eve's Fall

"When the woman saw that the fruit of the tree was good for food and pleasing to the eye, and also desirable for gaining wisdom, she took some and ate it" (Gen. 3:6).

Eve found herself longing with her eyes, lusting with her flesh, and falling prey to the pride of life. Her eyes found worth in the fruit, her senses told her that the fruit was good to eat, and her ambitions convinced her that she would gain new-found freedom.

In the same way, when many of us sin, it is out of these three reasons: the lust of the eyes, the lust of the flesh, and the pride of life (1 John 2:16). This occurs when we allow our sinful senses, rather than the Word of God, to control us. Then we choose what is harmful over what is good, in spite of God's warning.

Nature vs Nurture

One of the most common debates among theological, philosophical, and sociological circles concerns that of nature versus nurture. Are people born with wickedness in them (nature) or does their environment/upbringing turn them wicked (nurture)? When addressing this question, apologist Ravi Zacharias provided a witty response. He suggested that if wickedness were the results of a person's environment, when they commit crimes, we should imprison the perpetrators' neighbors rather than the perpetrators themselves. After all, they are to blame for the wickedness because of the environment they created.

The truth is that Eve lived in a perfect environment, and she still sinned. Thus, it is not our environment that truly has the final word; rather it is our desire to supplant all authority. This desire was conceived in Eve and passed through the generations. This malicious desire originated as a thought Satan proposed to Eve, a thought which Eve failed to hold captive. Let us not be like Eve. Rather, let us follow the example Paul outlines in his letter to the church at Corinth. "We demolish arguments and every pretension that sets itself up against the knowledge of God, and we take captive every thought to make it obedient to Christ" (2 Cor. 10:5). For it is our thoughts that lead to our actions.

Conclusion

In the wake of the Genesis account, "the Tree of the Knowledge of Good and Evil" has often been viewed in a negative light. In reality, though, the tree was pure and untouched by evil. The fruit itself was not evil, the sin was. Who knows, perhaps, had Eve obeyed God's command, He would have eventually allowed her to eat of that tree as well. The same is true today whereby we see

God as withholding a prize from us, when God knows that the right thing in the wrong season can lead to injury. What Eve saw as restricting her freedom was the very foundation of her liberty. By removing her obstacle and trespassing God's holy command, she exchanged her freedom for shackles. She ate the fruit before it was ripe! Fruit eaten before its proper season leads to sickness; thus, it was not that the fruit was rotten. It just was not yet ripe.

Unfortunately, Eve bought into Satan's lie that true paradise was not one where God reigned sovereign, but one where mankind ruled without restraint. Even today, we see the effects of this ideology throughout our culture. Eve was deceived through false speech and flattering lips. She may not have been made aware of Satan's existence prior to her encounter with the serpent, but even though she did not know who *he* was, she knew who God was. Even if she never heard a lie before, she was familiar with the truth.

Never once does God call us to fight the devil alone. Rather, He gives us everything we need to combat the serpent in the form of His Word. To this end, God gives us hope that the day will come when sin is eradicated, when all temptations end, for God Himself will handle the devil. To this end, God sent His Son that He might destroy the works of the devil. In speech and deed, Jesus did what Eve could not, and sure enough, after forty days of temptation, the devil fled from Jesus.

The power by which Jesus caused Satan to flee is the same power He provided to Eve and to all of us: the power of His Word. The devil came from his fallen place to steal, kill, and destroy, but Jesus (the Living Word) came down to give us life, and to give it to us abundantly. Praise God that the Way Up came down!

IV: THE FALL OF ADAM

Date: Earth's Early Years
Location: The Garden of Eden

Dumbstruck, Adam stared at the fruit in his wife's hand. It all transpired so quickly. He trusted Eve enough to know how to conduct herself in his absence, but in the moment of their separation, she chose to take the word of a serpent rather than her husband or God's word.

The serpent was nothing special. Adam named him along with all the other animals. All creatures that crawled, galloped, and scampered across the earth were subjected under his authority. Even the mammoths and tigers submitted to his commands. How could Eve have taken the advice of a lowly creature over which God had given them authority?

Listening to his wife's explanation, Adam felt his heart break inside him. He knew all that she said to be a lie. He was not deceived. He saw through the serpent's deception to the core of the temptation. He knew the serpent's words to be full of foolishness and guile. But what did it matter? His wife had already eaten the fruit. Now, what must he do?

Made for One Another

While the Bible is very clear regarding Eve's motives that led her to eat the fruit, there is no such clarity concerning Adam's motives. Often theologians mistranslate the phrase that Adam was "with her" during her temptation to refer to a physical interpretation, *i.e.*, that he was standing beside her. The Hebrew, though, implies an intimate interpretation from this phrase. Adam was Eve's husband, and the two were of one flesh. Never before was there a marriage like theirs. They were *literally* made for one another. It is in this sense that he was "with her," being of one accord.

Often among Christian circles, young people like to say that their significant other "completes" them, but the only couple that ever found a complement in each other was Adam and Eve. Adam was unable to find a suitable partner among the animals, thus, God made from his rib a woman.

When Adam saw Eve he said, "Wooooo, man! Woman!" or so the legends say. In all seriousness, Eve was in every way a suitable spouse for Adam. Many people like to imagine that there is a special someone waiting out there for them, but in the case of Adam, God specifically and purposely made that special someone for him! The two were joined together, and for a time, their marriage was sweeter than any other shall be. There was no strife, no jealousy, no arguing, no animosity, only love and trust, or so Adam thought.

Openness

It is important, especially in relationships, to be open with one another. If Eve had misgivings, she should have voiced her concerns with Adam or even God. Instead, we see that she takes matters into her own hands.

This is, honestly, how many of us choose to operate. Rather than share with God or our loved ones our struggles, we bottle them inside. The problem with this is that eventually whatever is inside will burst out. Truthfully, many people are embarrassed to come out and confess their misgivings not because they do not desire accountability, but because they are afraid of chastisement. Many Christians are quick to cast judgment when Jesus Himself said, "Do not judge, or you too will be judged" (Matt. 7:1). By the same measurement with which we judge others, we too will be judged. Thus, Jesus advocates that we approach people with grace and truth. If people are not open to you concerning their struggles, perhaps it is because they fear your resentful response.

As Christians, we need to be approachable to others, sharing the same love Jesus showed us. This does not mean, however, that if people choose not to reveal their struggles that it is entirely our fault. Eve was struggling inwardly whether or not Adam knew it. She was not open with her husband, and the doubts she kept bottled up spewed out.

How did Adam feel when she confronted him, apple in hand? Betrayed? Overlooked? Grieved? She did not consult him before making her decision. Instead of keeping the serpent on hold and seeking out the wisdom of her spouse, she chose to assume superiority in the relationship and to take independent action.

Perhaps Adam felt betrayed and indignant, but at the same time, his curiosity was piqued. God had said that should Adam or his wife eat of the fruit, they would perish. Yet, here stood Eve healthy as ever. What did this mean?

Guiles of a Woman

Satan's seduction of Eve was pivotal in causing Adam to sin. The Bible clearly states that "Adam was not the one deceived; it was the woman who was deceived and became a sinner" (1 Tim. 2:14). Maybe Satan knew that he could not deceive Adam through any sorts of trickery, and thus, he used Eve as a puppet to get to Adam. Regardless, when Eve approached Adam, she was a sinner and he was still holy.

Eve now possessed not only the experiential knowledge of goodness but also the experiential knowledge of evil. She sinned, and she liked it. It was a good feeling, so good in fact that it made her want to get her husband to follow in her footsteps. Have you ever noticed this? Sin loves company, and sinners especially love to be around other sinners.

In the end, Adam chose to listen to his wife instead of obeying God. He loved the gift more than the Gift-Giver, the creation more than the Creator. He fell because he chose to please a woman rather than to please God. In a sense, he committed adultery. He broke his relationship with God to pursue a relationship with another.

God warns multiple times for us not to allow our hearts to lead us astray. Calls to not be unevenly yoked and to avoid sexual promiscuity go unheeded as Christian men and women get caught up in their feelings. Feelings are a gauge, not a guide. They tell us the state of our heart but are not meant to direct our decisions. Feelings can be deceiving as well as fleeting, but God's word is truth and remains forever. It may not be what we want to hear, but it is what we need to hear. For the truth will set us free.

Sadly, many of us have become like Adam. We have abandoned our relationship with God to satisfy our relationship with another. Whether that other be a person or an addiction, it will hinder us from drawing closer to God.

Failed Guardian

So, what should have Adam done? If I were in Adam's shoes, I would like to think that I would have asked Eve further concerning the serpent. "Who is this guy?" I would have asked her. "Who's trying to meddle with my wife? Show me the man!"

Satan is the ultimate seducer, and his temptation of Eve was just that. It was a subtle seduction. Husbands are called to defend their wives. Thus, Adam should have confronted the serpent, as was his job. When God placed Adam in the Garden, He made Adam "keeper" of the Garden. The Hebrew word for keeper literally means "guard." Adam was to guard the Garden, but from what? From external forces of evil such as Satan. That Satan made it into the Garden without Adam's notice shows a possible lack of awareness on Adam's part.

How would you react if you found your wife conspiring with another, going against the very thing you warned her about? You would probably be rightly jealous and indignant! A husband ought to protect his wife, and while Adam could not have controlled Eve's actions, he could control his own.

The godly thing to do would be for him to petition God to spare his wife. Instead, Adam decides to seal his fate with hers. In this manner, he dooms the human race.

Federal Headship

Nearly every Christian, at some point, has found the concept that Adam's sin should affect us all to be unfair. Why should one man's sin count against all of us?

Federal (or seminal) headship, that of a male representing his descendants, is prevalent throughout Scripture. In Hebrews, the writer connects the tithing of Abraham with that of his son, Levi. "One might even say that Levi, who collects the tenth, paid the tenth through Abraham, because when Melchizedek met Abraham, Levi was still in the body of his ancestor" (Heb. 7:9-10). In this manner, Abraham represents his son, Levi, who is not even born yet.

Likewise, Adam represented all his descendants in the Garden. Every single human being can trace his or her lineage back to Adam. Thus, Romans says, "Therefore, just as sin entered the world through one man, and death through sin, and in this way death came to *all* people, because *all* sinned" (Rom. 5:12) (emphasis added).

"Well, we should have had a better representative," many have argued. To be fair, Adam was in truth the best we had to offer! As far as we know, he went the longest of any human being without sin, existing before Eve and having sinned after she did. Adam was a rarity. He had the constant opportunity to sin, and yet he chose not to. There is no other person, not Moses, David, or even Abraham, who could have made a better substitute. Adam was the pinnacle of human perfection, and yet even he fell. Adam was the closest any of us have ever come to perfection, and yet even he proved culpable. When he cast his vote in favor of rebellion, he voted on all our behalf.

Original Sin

The Bible says simply concerning Adam's fall, "[Eve] also gave some to her husband, who was with her, and he ate it" (Gen. 3:6). To Eve's credit, she did not use Adam as a guinea pig. Rather, she tested it herself before giving him the fruit. Yet, the moment Adam ate the fruit, he plunged the world into sin, affecting not only himself but all his descendants. His sin became hereditary, a deformed nature passed down through the generations to all people.

Ironically enough, a great many pastors disagree with the concept of original or imputed sin. "People are basically good!" they argue. But is this really true?

One day in English class, my professor was giving a dissertation when he brought up the basic goodness of people. Raising my hand, I asked my professor, "If most people are basically good, then how come there is violence in the world?"

My professor was stumped by this question. He did not know how to answer it. I went on to point out that even babies do not need to be taught selfishness, or youths how to lie. No one sends a child to a class where they learn bad manners or how to talk back to their parents. It is something they possess when they are youngsters. How can someone look at an atrocity such as the Holocaust and continue to labor under the delusion that most people are inherently good? There is obviously a problem in the world, so where did it come from?

The Bible traces the origin of all sin and suffering to Adam's disobedience in the Garden. As previously stated, Romans 5:12 makes it perfectly clear that sin entered the world on account of one man, that being Adam. A careful study of Scripture following Genesis 3 reveals the steady decline of the human race to the point where evil runs rampant, and God sends a worldwide flood to cleanse the wicked (Gen. 7).

Nevertheless, on account of Adam's sin, every one of us possesses an innate predisposition towards sin. No longer are we like Adam, who was born sinless, rather sin resides in us as a consequence of Adam's decision. Thus, we are not sinners because we sin. Rather, we sin because we are sinners. Adam's sin has been imputed to us, charged to our account. And so, our great champion became our great downfall.

The Immediate Effect

"Then the eyes of both of them were opened, and they realized they were naked; so they sewed fig leaves together and made coverings for themselves" (Gen. 3:7).

The effects of Adam and Eve's sin immediately settled upon the Garden. While as before, they never had reason to fear, they now felt their spirits tremble, for they knew they had done wrong. The knowledge of good and evil that they had gained from eating of the fruit pointed to an undeniable fact: The act they had just committed was evil.

Upon registering that they were naked, Adam and Eve felt shame in their nakedness and covered themselves. It is good for an individual to feel the shame of their sin, for those who have no shame allow themselves to be blindly controlled by sin, but those who see clearly that what they did was wrong, allow themselves the possibility of returning to the light.

In shame, Adam and Eve covered themselves, concealing the beauty of the Creator. Despite the great shame they felt for their nakedness, it was minuscule compared to their fear. What would God do to them? He told them plainly that if they ate from the fruit, they would surely perish!

Seconds turned into minutes and minutes turned into hours. Still, God did not show up. Yet, the longer the absence of God, the greater the fear of punishment swelled in Adam and Eve's hearts.

All the while, the serpent remained with them. Perhaps even now he was whispering further words of consultation. Or, perhaps he was berating them on behalf of their foolishness and disobedience. In either case, Satan wanted to stick around for the fireworks.

God had cast him from Heaven, and now Satan successfully turned God's prized creation against Him. Satan desired nothing more than to see how God would react. Would God save what he loved (Adam and Eve) and, therefore, at the same time, save what He hated (sin)? Or would He punish what He hated (sin), and in the same breath, punish what He loved (Adam and Eve)? Either way, God's decision would alter the course of history.

Conclusion

Over time, the common saying has developed that "the devil made me do it!" Oftentimes, we give the devil more clout than he actually has. The devil cannot infringe upon our free will. He cannot force us to do anything. Satan was unable to deceive Adam. The devil did not shove the fruit down his throat, rather he chose to approach Adam through another. Just as God uses people for his end means, so does Satan. Thus, we cannot entirely blame Satan for the fall. Adam ate willingly, indicating that even if Satan never tempted him, Adam would still have chosen to disobey God's perfect law.

Adam was like a fish who decided one day that he wanted to be free from the restrictive ocean. Hopping out of the water, the fish found that the freedom he formerly envisioned was not what he thought it would be. Likewise, the "freedom" Adam sought to obtain came at a price. In his sin, Adam doomed the human race. Each one of us bears the results of his actions. In desperation, the human race cried out to God. "We need a better representative!" humanity pleaded. "Adam was the best we had to offer, and he was still not good enough. We need a new Adam, a better Adam!"

In his letter to the Church in Rome, the Apostle Paul revealed the identity of humanity's new representative, one who surpassed Adam in every way.

> For if, by the trespass of the one man, death reigned through that one man, how much more will those who receive God's abundant provision of grace and of the gift of righteousness reign in life through the one man, Jesus Christ!
>
> Romans 5:17

While Adam failed to defend both his wife and him from sin, Jesus came down from Heaven to teach us how a son obeys and a loving husband stands up for His beloved. His death was not merely equal to the payment of sin, for Adam's sin required atonement only from one like Adam. Any perfect human being would do, but there could be found not one righteous person (Rom. 3:10). Thus, God Himself acted as our substitute. The infinite God laying down His life for humanity not only satisfied sin's ransom, but Jesus' death far surpassed it in every way. That is why we have this confidence: that the grace offered through Jesus is so much greater than the sin ushered in by Adam (Rom. 5:20). Jesus achieved what human representation never could and became for us our new federal head. We are His seed, His children, heirs of righteousness and friends of the one true King.

V: GARDENS INTO CITIES

Date: Early Years of Earth
Location: The Garden of Eden

Darkness clutched Adam's heart as his fingers relinquished the fruit. The once sweet juices of the fruit turned sour in his stomach. His insides churned as vomit rose to his lips. Puking out the grotesque substance he gawked at the red liquid mingled with his vomit. Was that...blood? It was! It was *his* blood!

Whipping around towards Eve, Adam found an expression of absolute terror etched across her once beautiful face. At a loss for words, Eve covered her mouth in horror. What had she done? Not only had she condemned herself, but she had condemned her husband with her. How would God respond? Would they be reduced to the dust from which they came?

Adam and Eve did not have a naive view of God wherein He would smile at them, pat them on the head, and wave His magic wand, removing the effects of their sin. They were aware that their choice deserved consequences, for they were acquainted with the nature of God. He already knew that they had eaten from the tree of which He had warned them not to. And they could neither stay His hand nor overpower Him to prevent His punishment. Thus, in fear and trembling, they waited on the Lord.

Cover Up

Upon eating the forbidden fruit, "Then the eyes of both of them were opened, and they realized they were naked; so they sewed fig leaves together and made coverings for themselves" (Gen. 3:7). The sin of Adam and Eve caused them to feel shame, a feeling they had never experienced before. Thus, in an attempt to cope with their shame, they made coverings for themselves.

A cover up is the first step in the downward trajectory of a failing spiritual life. In a cover up, one attempts to hide his wrongdoing in plain sight. For this to work, an individual will go to extreme lengths to conceal his deeds, lest they be exposed. In the case of Adam and Eve, they used fig leaves, which ironically are known to irritate the skin. Thus, they compromised themselves further to attempt to remedy their situation.

Today's world is no different. Instead of coming clean and confessing our sins, many Christians commit a spiritual cover up. We foolishly attempt to hide our deeds from others, but God sees it all and the Bible makes it clear that your sin will find you out (Num. 32:23). Therefore, the shame which originally was intended to motivate you towards repentance now turns into guilt.

Shame is a good thing. Had Adam and Eve not felt any shame regarding their sin, there could be no possibility of change. The very fact that we feel shame when we sin identifies hope in our spiritual life. We are not too far gone. There is still time to confess and repent, to take off the guise with which we have adorned ourselves, to remove the fig leaves, and to own up to our sin. But if we try to maintain the guise, beware. "For the word of God is alive and active. Sharper than any double-edged sword, it penetrates even to dividing soul and spirit, joints and marrow; it judges the thoughts and attitudes of the heart" (Heb. 4:12). You may fool men, but you cannot fool God. In the end, He will strip away every ruse, every covering and lay bare the deeds of all men.

A Somber Welcome

"Then the man and his wife heard the sound of the Lord God as He was walking in the garden in the cool of the day, and they hid from the Lord God among the trees of the garden" (Gen. 3:8).

God waited until the cool of the day, right before the darkness of night. Showing mercy to His children, God refused to prolong their waiting, resigning not to leave them trembling in the shadows. Instead, God showed up in their midst in the form of His Son, Jesus (a christophany).[3]

God often walked with Adam and Eve at this time of day, but today was different. Often, they came to Him happy to see Him, but not this day. What hindered them from coming to God? What prevented them from drawing near to Him?

This was the most somber greeting God had experienced up to this time. Usually, whenever He appeared, angels marveled and bowed down and Adam and Eve jumped for joy; but when God walked through Eden that day, He walked alone. No one came looking for Him, and no one rejoiced at the sound of His coming. Rather, each one turned to his or her own way.

Running from God

The second step in the downward trajectory of a failing spiritual life is to run from God. In fear and despair, Adam and Eve tried to escape the presence of the King of Heaven. Tears stained their faces as they attempted to flee from the One whom they had once cherished. He was their greatest friend, their wisest counselor, but their perspective had changed. He had now become their greatest enemy, the object of their fear and mistrust.

As they raced to avert Him, God, who sees all things, perceived their actions. His eyes traced them through the trees of His making. It broke His heart to see His children desperate to avoid Him, their good and loving Father.

In that moment, God could have justly struck both of them dead. He could have ended their lives on the spot and formed two new human beings from the dust of the Earth. But He chose not to. Nor did He simply turn His back on Adam and Eve and consign them to the horrors of fear and shame.

Had God never confronted Adam and Eve with their sin, they would have continued to live with regret until their last dying breath. Unconfronted sin gives birth to shame, regret, and guilt; but when sin is laid bare, God can use His redemptive powers to cleanse us from all unrighteousness (1 John. 1:9).

Running from God is the first step towards seeking to avoid judgment. Many people live this way as refugees, attempting to keep themselves at a distance from God. Unfortunately, the Psalmist made known the impossibility of fleeing from God's presence. "Where can I go from your Spirit? Where can I flee from your presence? If I go up to the heavens, you are there; if I make my bed in the depths, you are there" (Ps. 139:7-8). The omnipresence of God is what makes every human being tremble. For Him to be omnipresent means that He perceives all that is done. Just as He saw Nathanael under the fig tree, so He sees each and every wicked deed we commit.

Knowing this, Adam and Eve resolve not simply to run from God but to pursue the next course of action involved in a spiritual cover-up: concealment.

Hide and Seek

The third step in the downward trajectory of a failing spiritual life is to attempt to hide from God. This occasion when Adam and Eve hid themselves from God was the first ever recorded version of hide-and-seek in the Bible. Adam and Eve not only fled from God, but they attempted to conceal themselves behind God's own creation. Did they really believe God did not know where they were? How foolish to hide from an omniscient God, right?

We, too, though, can be guilty of similar foolishness. Sometimes we attempt to mask our true natures, our inner desires, and the sin of our hearts by covering these things up with a facade of godliness – as if we could hide from God. God, however, is able to see through the veil. Man looks on outwards things, but God perceives the heart (1 Sam. 16:7). Our true selves are laid bare before Him.

"Nothing in all creation is hidden from God's sight. Everything is uncovered and laid bare before the eyes of him to whom we must give account" (Heb. 4:13). Men like Jonah have attempted to put God to the test, but God proved that you can attempt to run from Him, but you cannot hide. He saw Jonah board the boat bound for Tarshish, just as He saw Adam and Eve hidden amongst the trees.

The omnipresence of God should cause men to think, act, and speak differently since He who sees all things will call us to give an account. None of our deeds are concealed. Nothing we do goes unseen. "'Who can hide in secret places so that I cannot see them?' declares the LORD. 'Do not I fill heaven and earth?' declares the LORD" (Jer. 23:24). God witnesses it all, and He records our every lie, every theft, every thought to the letter, and when He comes for us seeking justice, there is nowhere for us to hide.

Ready or not, here He comes! His eyes roamed to and fro, but He knew where Adam and Eve cowered. At last, God opened His mouth. God did not address Eve. He addressed the man whom He placed over the Garden.

"[T]he Lord God called to the man, 'Where are you?'" (Gen. 3:9).

Adam was discovered! God's cry shook Adam to his core. He felt shame for having disappointed his gracious Creator, and he felt fear for what God might do to him on account of his actions. Nevertheless, Adam spoke up. He realized he could not run or hide forever. The only way he could remove this feeling of shame was to step into the light.

Lizard Brain

Timidly emerging from behind the trees, Adam stood in full view of his Creator. Trembling, Adam laid himself at the mercy of God. "He answered, 'I heard you in the garden, and I was afraid because I was naked; so I hid'" (Gen. 3:10).

God responded to Adam in the form of questions. "And he said, 'Who told you that you were naked? Have you eaten from the tree that I commanded you not to eat from?'" (Gen. 3:11). Satan started off his conversation with Eve with questioning, hoping that his queries would lead to doubt. In sharp contrast, God utilized questions to lead to confession and repentance.

Fascinatingly, scientists call the limbic cortex, the part of the brain responsible for many of our emotional processings, the "lizard brain." The reason being, this part of the brain operates in the same manner that a lizard's brain does. A lizard's brain does not have the capacity to contemplate actions other than the four Fs: fight, flight, feeding, and fear. The lizard brain also is the pessimistic part of the brain that urges us towards selfish actions and convinces us of our inabilities. "You're not a good ball player." "You don't have what it takes to be a single mother." "God doesn't love you." "You came from dust." "You're worthless in His sight."

The lizard brain is synonymous to the voices of Satan and his minions. Adam and Eve allowed themselves to fall prey to this lizard brain, to the temptations of the evil one. As a result, billions of people today hear the lying voice of Satan telling them they will never make it. They will never be enough.

That is why when God confronts Adam, He gets Adam to check the voices in his head. "Who told you you were naked?" To whom had Adam been listening? Is his counselor God, or this serpent? What voices are influencing him and his perception of the world? The source of the voice reveals the relative trustworthiness of the words. This holds true for Adam and even for us today.

The Blame Game

Rather than own up to his sin, Adam attempts to deflect responsibility. He cowered after he ate the fruit, and he cowered again when God questioned him. "The man said, 'The woman you put here with me — she gave me some fruit from the tree, and I ate it'" (Gen. 3:12).

Shirking his duty, Adam quickly diverts attention away from himself. Not only does Adam blame Eve, but he also blames God for his trouble. He accuses Eve as the one who caused him to sin and God as the one who placed her in the Garden with him. Adam did not request Eve's presence, rather, God made Eve for Adam. Thus, Adam insinuates that God was partially to blame.

"Then the Lord God said to the woman, 'What is this you have done?'

The woman said, 'The serpent deceived me, and I ate'" (Gen. 3:13).

Following her husband's example, Eve shifts blame to the serpent. Okay, so who is left for the serpent to blame? No one. Satan acted on his own accord, without external prompting. Thus, God does not even bother to question Satan. He knows from what motives Satan operates, and He does not bother to give Satan the opportunity to repent or the satisfaction of speaking a sentence in His presence.

The first individual God punishes is not Adam and Eve, but Satan. God realizes that he is the one who set in motion the whole chain of events leading to the fall of man, and thus God curses him.

The *Protoevangelium*

God says to Satan, "And I will put enmity between you and the woman, and between your seed and her seed; He shall bruise you on the head, and you shall bruise him on the heel" (Gen. 3:15, NASB).

This sentence is known as the *protoevangelium*, the first Gospel. Here, God promises hope to mankind and defeat to Satan. The first promise God makes to humanity is that of enmity He will cause between Satan and the woman. Formerly, the two were of one mind, opposed to God. However, God Himself will rectify this unholy alliance. For Eve's own good, He will cause her to see Satan for who He is. Likewise, in our own lives, God will occasionally lift the blinders from our eyes so that we may see the enemy for who he is. Just as God opened the eyes of Elisha's servant, so He opens the eyes of many to see past the devil's schemes. Only when people see the devil for who he is do they shudder and resist his detestable ploys.

Not only will Eve be at enmity with Satan, but so will her descendants. The people of God will strive against the allies of Satan. In the following chapters of Genesis, we see this struggle manifest where the unrighteous persecute and purge the righteous. But God promises further hope. He tells the woman that the seed of her womb will crush the devil.

Interestingly, God uses the term "seed" to refer to the woman's offspring. A woman is known to possess eggs, while a man bears the seed. In this case, however, God refers to the *woman's* seed. This is unmistakably the first prophecy concerning the virgin birth of Jesus. God's seed (Jesus) would be planted in Mary, and the Holy Spirit would conceive Him that He might set the world free from sin's fatal curse.

Jesus did not jump on the scene in Bethlehem, several thousand years later. Rather, He was the one in the Garden who confronted Adam and Eve, and He was the one He promised would rectify humanity's sin. Jesus was foretold from the beginning, for hope was given the moment fear entered the world. Fear does not have the last word. Hope does, and God extended this hope to Adam and Eve.

Additionally, Jesus Himself later told a relevant prophecy about Himself as a seed. He explained, "Very truly I tell you, unless a kernel of wheat falls to the ground and dies, it remains only a single seed. But if it dies, it produces many seeds" (John 12:24). Jesus, the promised Seed, was planted when He was buried in the earth for three days. He then emerged as the first-fruits, the firstborn among many brethren (Rom. 8:29). Jesus was the Seed that yielded the righteous.

So how did Jesus bruise, or crush, Satan's head? By His death and resurrection. Jesus destroyed Satan's plan to ruin humanity. He rescued mankind from the grip of sin and death, which are Satan's weapons of mass destruction. Interestingly, the place of Jesus' crucifixion was known as "Golgotha," which means "the place of the skull." When Jesus' cross was thrust into the ground on Golgotha's, He was crushing Satan's head.

So, what about Satan's striking the heel of Eve's offspring? For someone to attack another's heel, the blow must be aimed low and from behind. The heel is within a serpent's range. Likewise, Jesus had to lower Himself to enter into Satan's domain that He might be smitten for the world's transgression.

Not only that, but the strike came from behind in the sense that much surrounding the circumstances of Jesus' death was twisted and devious, including the back-stabbing betrayal by Judas. Thus, Jesus suffered a bruised heel in the form of the crucifixion. Unlike a crushed head, though, a bruised heel is not a fatal injury.

Some have often wondered, "If Satan is crushed, then why does he still hold so much influence?" One must understand the nature of snakes to understand the crushing of Satan. I remember one hot summer day visiting an amusement park called Six Flags Great Adventure. As I was waiting in line for a ride, a small black snake darted out from under a nearby bush. Wild snake sightings were rare for a twelve-year-old New Jersey boy like myself, so I admit I did not shout with glee. Instantly, my older, Florida-raised friend Sean jumped down from the railing he was sitting on and crushed the snake with his foot. The snake was instantly killed, but for the next minute or so, I watched as it continued to squirm and writhe. It was crushed, but it was still enduring its death pains. Likewise, Satan has been crushed, but he is waiting out his death pangs.

Labor Pain

Justly, but unfortunately for Adam and Eve, God did not expunge their misdeeds. Rather, after punishing Satan, He continued to assign judgment to them. He first gave the good news, the promise of Satan's future defeat. Then came the bad news, which always follows sin.

"To the woman he said, 'I will make your pains in child-bearing very severe; with painful labor you will give birth to children'" (Gen. 3:16). The sentence God pronounces on the woman differs from that which He declares against the serpent. While God curses the serpent, He does not curse the woman. She is punished, but not cursed, chastised but loved.

The English Standard Version says that God will "multiply" Eve's pain in childbearing. In other words, she would already experience pain, but now that she has sinned, her pain shall be increased. While I have never given birth before, nor do I ever plan on it, I have spoken with a number of strong women who all undeniably affirm the extreme pain of child labor. My own mother gave birth to seven children, and each time, I am sure she was reminded of the consequence God imposed on Eve.

Even so, child labor pain may be viewed as a reminder of God's blessing. God could have created a new wife for Adam, or even a new set of parents, more qualified to parent children. Had Adam and Eve been interviewed by child protective services, they would hardly meet the necessary qualifications to raise a child. Making a deal with the devil and plunging the world into sin and death do not make for the best credentials. Yet, God, our Good Father, showed mercy to Eve that instead of closing her womb, He enabled her to have children. Among her descendants was God's own Son, born of the Virgin Mary (Matt. 1:16). So, while increased labor pains are the result of the fall, the very ability to give birth to children reflects God's goodness and mercy.

Fascinatingly enough, Eve is not called "Eve" until after the fall. Throughout the Genesis 3 narrative, she is known as "the woman," but after the fall, Adam names her "Eve," which means "the mother of all the living." God used a sinful, deceived woman like Eve and a sinful, rebellious man like Adam to begin the entire human race. If God could entrust children to a woman the likes of Eve and a man the likes of Adam, what is to hinder Him from using you? He has a purpose for your life, and He can achieve His plans even despite your past misdeeds. Thanks be to God for His incredible mercy!

Battle of the Sexes

In addition to increased labor pain, God's judgment against Eve permeated her relationship with Adam: "Your desire will be for your husband, and he will rule over you" (Gen. 3:16).

The Hebrew word for "desire" in this context does not refer to sexual or romantic desire, but instead that wives will seek to rule over their husbands. God is very clear in Scripture as to the role of husbands, wives, and children, but Satan has pointedly attacked the family. He incessantly tempts humanity with freedom akin to that he promised Eve if they will only usurp the place of another. Yet, despite Eve's desire for her husband's authority, God proclaimed that Adam would rule over her. God does not condone misogynistic treatment of women, but He does call for wives to submit themselves to their husbands (Eph. 5:22). Sin first entered the world when one man's wife failed to do such a thing, when the roles of husband and wife were reversed. The first attack Satan made against humanity was in the home, and to this day, his strategy has not changed.

Putting Adam in His Place

Following God's judgment of Eve, God turns to Adam and says,

Because you listened to your wife and ate fruit from the tree about which I commanded you, "You must not eat from it," Cursed is the ground because of you; through painful toil you will eat food from it all the days of your life. It will produce thorns and thistles for you, and you will eat the plants of the field.

Genesis 3:17-18

Unlike the serpent and unlike the woman, God offers an explanation for His judgment regarding Adam. God leaves no doubt as to why He is punishing him, for Adam was God's steward, and he failed in his task. Eve fell prey to Satan, and Adam followed the example of his wife. God did not call for Adam to listen to his wife. He told Adam to listen to Him! Whatever God says to do trumps any voice to the contrary. If a spouse or anyone else attempts to persuade you to infringe upon God's commands, you must unequivocally reject such demands lest you follow in Adam's footsteps.

Because of Adam, God cursed the very creation He had called good. Rather than curse the man, God treated the ground as a sort of substitutional whipping boy. In the medieval days, a prince could not be punished for his misconduct. Thus, a whipping boy was to incur the prince's punishment in his place. When the prince misbehaved, the whipping boy paid the price. Like an innocent whipping boy, the ground incurred God's wrath over Adam's sin.

But Adam was not off the hook. Because of the ground's curse, Adam's labor would prove wearisome, something I, as a summer landscaper, can attest to. Whenever I work outside in the scorching heat, tackling English Ivy, thorns, and thistles, I know who to blame for making my job so difficult. Thus, just as God exacerbated the pain of Eve's labor, He similarly increased the difficulty of Adam's labor.

Additionally, God delivered on the promise He made long ago regarding the ultimate consequence of eating the fruit. God told Adam that on account of his sin, he would indeed perish, returning to the dust from which God had formed him. "For dust you are, and to the dust you will return" (Gen. 3:19). In this manner, God reveals the innate worth of man apart from Him. Before God, man was dust, and without God, man shall be dust again. Upon death, all men shall become one with the cursed ground owing to Adam and Eve's attempted usurpation of God's place in Creation. Their actions were akin to the Earth demanding that the Sun revolve around it. Even if it were possible, such a request would prove terribly detrimental to the Earth. Likewise, humanity needs a God-centered way of life, otherwise we will face disastrous consequences. Either God is the center of it all, or He is not the center at all. There is no middle ground.

Clothed by God

Following God's declaration of judgment, "The Lord God made garments of skin for Adam and his wife and clothed them" (Gen. 3:21). To alleviate Adam and Eve's shame, God provided an appropriate covering for them. He did for them that which they were incapable of accomplishing for themselves.

He took Adam and Eve's nakedness and consequent shame and wrapped them in garments of His making. A proper covering required nothing less than a sacrificial death. So also, He promises that all those who repent of their sins and trust in Jesus' sacrificial death, professing Him as Lord and Savior, will exchange their filthy rags for robes of righteousness (Is. 61:10).

Expulsion

And the Lord God said, The man has now become like one of us, knowing good and evil. He must not be allowed to reach out his hand and take also from the tree of life and eat, and live forever." So the Lord God banished him from the Garden of Eden to work the ground from which he had been taken.

Genesis 3:22-23

Due to Adam and Eve's sin, they could no longer remain in the Garden, for God did not desire for mankind to eat of the Tree of Life and thus extend their days of torment. Instead, while death was the consequence for their disobedience, God also decreed it as a mercy to end the days people would be confined to live in a sinful world.

Taking Adam in one hand, and Eve in the other, God led them out of the Garden and into the world beyond. The Garden of Eden was mankind's home, just as Heaven was Satan's, but like Satan, Adam and Eve were forced from their home on account of their rebellion. Nevertheless, while the Garden of Eden was closed to mankind, guarded by God's cherubim (Gen. 3:24), God still had a plan for them and their descendants.

Conclusion

When God closed the Garden of Eden to Adam and Eve, He did not abandon them to damnation. Rather, He pursued the plan He established from the dawn of Creation. The Garden was only the beginning. God, in His foreknowledge, knew that Adam and Eve would fall into sin, as He knows each of us will sin. In His wisdom and His love, however, God prepared in advance a way for the citizens of Earth to dwell among the angels of Heaven.

In one of His parables, Jesus declares that those who do God's will are selected to join the angels in the heavenly kingdom. "Then the King will say to those on his right, 'Come, you who are blessed by my Father; take your inheritance, the kingdom prepared for you since the creation of the world'" (Matt. 25:34). Adam and his line could never again hope to return to the Garden, but God gave them hope that there was a way by which they could indeed reach the Heavenly City. Their sin deserved eternal damnation in Hell, apart from His presence, but instead God showed them mercy, promising that the Way up would come down.

To those who conquer, those who put their faith in this Way, in the Seed of the woman, God promises them fruit of another tree. For, in the Garden of Eden stood two wondrous trees: The Tree of the Knowledge of Good and Evil and the Tree of Life. Eating the former leads to death, but the sweet fruit of the latter leads to eternal life. Thus, God has placed this tree in the heavenly realm, the Restored Eden, where there is no curse, no banishment, no sin, no serpent, and no death. God is making all things new. The way to creative life is also the way to sustaining life. Satan tempted the woman to steal and eat, but God Himself allows us to take and eat, free of guilt and pain. We need not greedily snatch the fruit from the vine. Rather, God will pluck it Himself and hand it to us, for He, and He alone, is the way to the life of purpose and fulfillment we were made for.

PART TWO

Dead End: The Wrong Way

VI: TOWERS AND TONGUES

Date: c. 2242 BC
Location: Shinar

After popping another luscious grape into his mouth, Nimrod washed it down with a robust gulp of wine. The rich red juices trickled down his beard but were swiftly patted dry by one of Nimrod's doting attendants. Nimrod barely took notice, though, so fixated was he on the gargantuan ziggurat towering before him. Its top pierced the sky and it loomed above the clouds like a mountain of industry, dwarfing all else on the plain of Shinar. Despite its already impressive height, Nimrod continued the already decades-long construction process. He intended that, in its final stage, the tower of Babel would ascend to the very abode of God Himself.

To some, Nimrod feigned that the tower's creation existed to bring men into the presence of God, or to seek to bring God down. However, Nimrod had much more devious intentions. He, like all men, knew well the stories of the great Flood in which God had wiped out all civilizations to cleanse

the world of wickedness. While the peoples of the earth succumbed to the torrents of God's wrath, Nimrod refused to be
caught unawares and to suffer the same fate (despite God's
promise to Noah and his descendants that He would never
again flood the Earth).

Sparing no expense, he ordered the construction of a tower
designed to reach Heaven itself. Yet, Nimrod did not have the
necessary workers to complete his project. Thus, he dispatched
slave masters to the far reaches of his kingdom and drove thousands of his subjects to the plain of Shinar, where they began
to erect the tower of Babel.

As Nimrod watched his workers, he could see the anguish
and exhaustion expressed on their faces. Often, though, they
did not even require the lash of the taskmasters to motivate
them. The majority of the workers *wanted* to be there, they
wanted to work on the tower.

A wry smile crossed Nimrod's lips as he recalled the lie
he had spun to entrap his laborers. He convinced them that
obedience to God did not bring true happiness, but that true
happiness was a product of their own design. Thus, even when
women gave birth to children, they simply wrapped the child
up in their aprons and continued working, believing that their
involvement in the tower's construction would ultimately lead
to their happily ever after.

Crossing his arms in satisfaction and confident that he
would witness the fruit of his scheming, Nimrod relaxed on his
regal throne. He had overseen the tower's construction for the
past several decades, and in all that time he had not received
a single major interruption, whether from men or from God.
Thus, Nimrod mocked God in his heart believing that the

Almighty had relinquished His reign on the Earth, and that he, Nimrod, was the new ruler in charge.

The world was his footstool and all peoples lived to please him. He was Nimrod the Great, kingdom founder and city a maker (Gen. 10:11-12). He was the first of the prominent kings of Earth (Gen. 10:9-12) and a mighty hunter among men (Gen. 10:8-9). His enemies would live and die unnamed, but Nimrod's legacy would endure the test of time.

Consequence of the Fall

Many people examine the wicked, self-glorified life of Nimrod and the people of Babel, and they cannot help but wonder how humanity succumbed to such depravity. The Bible made it clear that on account of Adam and Eve's sin in the Garden, Creation was cursed, and mankind was now vulnerable both to the temptations and the penalty of sin. It got to a point where almost every human being on the planet was involved in absolute wickedness, with not a single thought dedicated to benevolence. Therefore, God unleashed the waterfalls of Heaven on the earth, purging all life except for those He shielded in Noah's ark.

God hoped to start anew with Noah, his family, and the animals on Noah's ark, but soon after Noah and the animals left the ark, humanity drifted back into sin. Like Adam's descendants, Noah's descendants fell away from worshipping God alone and instead sought to honor and worship themselves. Their narcissism eventually culminated in the construction of the infamous Tower of Babel.

No Other Gods

Perhaps nowhere else in Scripture was the counterfeit path of salvation better allegorically epitomized than in the Tower of Babel account. God made it crystal clear to Adam and later to Noah that salvation came only from the Lord, who reigned above; but Nimrod and his people, who reigned below, sought to work their way up. In this way, Nimrod established a new religious system in which he, the created object, became the center of worship.

This sin stood in direct contrast to God's very first command given to Moses: thou shalt have no other gods before me. Yet, throughout human existence, we see the attempt to remove God from the picture and to establish humanity as the supreme object of exaltation. Where does this desire to supplant God come from?

It all goes back to the Garden when Satan tempted Eve to eat of the fruit and become like God. Ever since then, human beings have tried to build themselves up to divine status, whether by believing they can truly become gods or by attempting to craft a deity according to their liking. In this way, mankind has also broken the second commandment, *i.e.*, creating an idol as their focus of worship.

Only One God

If one were to read only a brief account of history, one would quickly conclude that God does not deal kindly with men who claim to be gods. In Genesis 11, the Bible records that the people of Babel say, "Come, let us build ourselves a city, with a tower that reaches to the heavens, so that we may make a name for ourselves; otherwise we will be scattered over the face of the whole earth" (Gen. 11:4). Their decision not to scatter but to build a city and a tower was in direct defiance of God's command. This decision was not accidental but rather purposeful. The motivation for this sin is clear: "that we may make a name for ourselves[.]" In short, they were declaring themselves to be gods. They were not content to remain at the natural level God placed them, rather, they sought to usurp God's position for themselves.

This action reminds me of an infamous Greek myth concerning the hero Bellerophon. Widely known throughout Greece for his slaying of the beast, Chimera, Bellerophon was hailed amongst his peers as a god. Thinking himself equal with Zeus, Bellerophon bridled Pegasus, the Greek flying horse, and ascended to Mount Olympus, the abode of the gods. Zeus, perceiving Bellerophon's intent, dispatched a tiny insect which frightened Pegasus and sent Bellerophon tumbling downwards to his doom.

Likewise, God opposes those who seek to supplant Him. He is holy, and those who attempt to usurp His place will be cast down as an example to others. Thus, with righteous zeal to defend His own, God noticed and responded to the people of Babel's wicked deed: "But the LORD came down to see the city and the tower the people were building" (Gen. 11:5).

Nimrod and the people of Shinar attempted to build a tower to Heaven, but it was so puny compared to the eternal God that, to get on the same level as the tower, God had to come down. Thus, human beings can attempt to become like God, but they will never be Him. And whenever this occurs, God often responds by thwarting the plans of these would-be gods, these pretenders of divinity.

Forsaking God

Did God need to come down to see the city and the tower? Of course not. God in His power could perceive the city and the tower to their most minuscule details from the outermost reaches of space. But because He plays an active role in the affairs of men, God chose to come down from on high.

How unfortunate, though, that when God descended, no one perceived it. They had become so fixated on the works of their hands that they did not even notice that the *God who formed them with His hand* was in their midst. Amazingly, blinded by the things of the world and focused on their own agenda, they did not even realize their very Creator was among them.

How sad it is that God's own Creation would miss out on Him because they are too preoccupied with their own creations. Yet, how often does this occur still today? How many times do we allow a screen or a hobby or just busyness to take away from time that could be spent with God? How often do we choose to watch, play, or even read something else instead of opening His Word? Before we condemn the people of Babel for not noticing when God showed up, we must answer honestly if we ourselves are even looking for Him.

An Effective Discipline

The people of Babel wanted nothing to do with the true God. Rather than thanking Him for His continued mercy, they shunned Him. They spitefully disobeyed His law and sought to replace Him with themselves.

Although grieved, God did not give man over to their depravity. He did not allow them to continue down their path of rebellion like they did in the time of Noah. Rather, God said:

If as one people speaking the same language they have begun to do this, then nothing they plan to do will be impossible for them. Come, let us go down and confuse their language so they will not understand each other.

Genesis 11:6-7

In His mercy, God did not consume humanity as He had before. Instead, He merely confused their language. He could have sent a plague, or even an angel to smite them. He could have shown up in their midst and forced every one of them to their knees. Yet He chose to achieve His purpose with tremendous grace.

God identified the root of the city, its very foundation. Everything the people of Babel were able to do was based solely on their ability to communicate with one another at large. If stripped of this ability, the people would cease their work on the tower. If God did not thwart their work, however, as God himself incredibly admitted, nothing they set their minds to could be stopped.

Many theologians who read this statement scoff, claiming that God's statement about human ability should not be taken literally. But is that so? Look at what has happened over the course of history when only a fraction of humanity has put their minds together. Electricity, space travel, nuclear weapons, and real-time communication across the globe are just some of the astounding developments achieved by human beings.

This was all accomplished because a few minds came together. Let us suppose that all barriers were stripped, and we were united once more with one language and one vision. What could we not do? Even the very sky is not the limit for human beings.

Knowing this truth, *i.e.*, that if humanity remained under one language, they could do unlimited great and terrible things, God caused there to be division of tongues among the people of Babel. This miraculous expression of God's power was both effective and beautiful. It was effective because through it, God achieved His purpose: the people spread out on the earth (as He had commanded them to do in the first place). It was also beautiful, because God could have chosen a number of ways to disperse the people, but He did so without destroying a single soul. He also did not diminish their intellectual capacity. Instead, He instantaneously created a host of new languages. God did not reduce mankind to a state of ignorance whereby their linguistic skills were lesser than before. Rather, God created a series of entirely developed, new languages whereby groups of men and women could effectively communicate with one another.

How was this possible? How did God place these languages in their minds? How did the people speak, and yet pronounce words differently than they intended to? Or how did they think in new words? The miracle of God achieved at Babel cannot be overstated in its complexity and beauty, for He imparted a gift as a farewell present to the people. They were leaving Shinar, but they would not go empty handed.

Instantly, work on the tower abruptly halted as the people could no longer understand one another. And so, they dropped their stones and began to scatter – just as God had commanded in the first place. The stones of defiance that they used to build both their city and their tower tumbled out of their hands as the people dispersed across the earth, in accordance with God's will.

Let Us

The Tower of Babel account teaches many important theological lessons, a principal one of which centers on man's ultimate desire of unseating God and God's refusal to step off the throne. This is evident in the universal language utilized throughout Genesis. Twice the people of Shinar say, "Let us," invoking their unified interests in opposition against God. But God has the last word.

The first biblical mention of the phrase "let us" occurs in Genesis 1:26 where God makes known His desire to make an image of Himself. "Then God said, *'Let us* make mankind in our image, in our likeness'" (Gen. 1:26) (emphasis added). The second biblical mention of this phrase occurs in the Babel account where mankind desires to make an image for themselves. "Come, *let us* build ourselves a city, with a tower that reaches to the heavens, *so that we may make a name for ourselves*" (Gen. 11:4) (emphasis added). Thus, while the first use of this phrase in Scripture refers to a unity for the purpose of harmony in glorifying God, the second usage refers to a unity for the purpose of rebellion against Him.

Thankfully, the third usage of the phrase "let us" occurs in this very same passage as the second one. In response to the people's intentions to unite together to replace God, the Father calls on the Trinity to take action once more for the wellbeing of mankind. "Come, *let us* go down and confuse their language so they will not understand each other" (Gen. 11:7) (emphasis added).

When I was younger, my siblings and I would often quarrel, and the rule of thumb was that whoever said "period" won the argument. There was nothing you could say after the period rule had been invoked. In the same way, God invoked the period rule on the people of Babel. God said, "Let us," then the people of Babel said, "Let us," but then (to paraphrase) God said, "You don't get to say, 'Let us'! That's outside of your jurisdiction. Only I get to say, 'Let us.' Period."

Nimrod and his subjects sought to do one thing, but God's sovereign will impeded their purpose. While there are many times in which God allows mankind to go its way, there are some occasions where God inserts Himself into humanity's situation out of His love and compassion. He could have left the people of Babel to their own devices, blotting them from His mind, or He could have sent a plague or natural disaster as judgment for their disobedience. Yet, rather than pursue either of these harsh, yet just, courses of action, God mercifully chose a way whereby He bloodlessly achieved His intentions. Every life was spared so that all might bear witness to the truth that the God of Heaven is Lord of all the earth, and none can stay His hand or plot against His will.

Conclusion

While the physical Tower of Babel may have crumbled long ago, the spiritual Babel prevails to this day. The temptation to build a city and a tower as one people, united in purpose, tempts not only unbelievers but believers alike. Evangelical leaders often attempt to coerce the varied denominations of Christianity to join together along with other major world religions. Yet, the God who separated the people of Babel to achieve His purpose is the same God who refuses to allow His Name and purpose to be defiled.

God gave a command for the church to place Him at the center, just like He commanded the people of Babel; but instead of obeying, the religious crowd put man at the center. They created a man-made religion and attempted to coerce all humanity to engage in this wicked religion or perish. It is time today in America and around the world that the church remembers that God is at the center of it all. We do not put Him there. We do not make Him the center. He is the center! We simply acknowledge it and live our lives in light of this truth.

Similarly, for centuries, the Roman Catholic Church taught that the earth was the center of the universe, and that the sun and all the planets revolved around it. This geocentric view was challenged by many, especially one man named Galileo. Through scientific evidence, Galileo pointed to the fact that the Sun was the center, and that the earth and all the planets revolved around it. We need a heliocentric revolution in our own lives! We need to remember that the Son is at the center, not us, and that in many cases, this will be cause for division. Yet, we do not compromise. Instead, we hold fast to the truth that was revealed to us, knowing that the day approaches when we shall be judged according to our confession. How will God judge us on that day? Will the door close before us, leaving us to wail outside, or will He welcome us to the feast with open arms?

VII: PILLARS AND PILLOWS

Date: c. 1929 BC
Location: Outside the city of Luz

The chilly evening breeze numbed Jacob's fingers as he drew his covering even more tightly over himself. Jacob refused to lodge with the people of the nearby desert town because of their devotion to idols, so now he lacked the luxury of a tent to protect him from the frigid nighttime conditions. Jacob was not cut from the same cloth as the people of Luz, rather, he was the grandson of Abraham, to whom was given the revelation of the one true God, *El Shaddai*, God Almighty. Thus, Abraham and his descendants worshipped God alone...or did they?

Jacob shivered once more, but this time, it was not because of the glacial evening wind. Rather, Jacob shifted uncomfortably upon considering the poor spiritual condition of his heart. One would have thought that at seventy-seven years old, Jacob would have gotten his act together, but he was still as selfish and conniving as when he was a teenager. In fact, he himself was to blame for his having to sleep alone outside in the wilderness with a pile of rocks for a pillow.

Not long ago, Jacob lived peacefully with his mother, Rebekah; his father, Isaac; and his brother, Esau. While Esau had three wives, two Canaanite and one Ishmaelite, Jacob remained single. Even in his old age, he gave no prospect of carrying on the family lineage or even showing interest in the possibility of marriage. Rather, he enjoyed the comforts of home and the doting attention of his mother, who fawned over him to no end.

Jacob was his mother's favorite son, and Esau was his father's favorite. Because of this, a wedge was driven between Jacob and his father as well as between Jacob and his brother. It did not help matters that Jacob lacked the motivation to work hard for anything, preferring instead to achieve his goals through craftiness.

Sure enough, through cunning planning and his mother's aid, Jacob managed not only to coax his brother Esau's birthright from him but also to snatch the family blessing. Nevertheless, all his scheming was for naught when Esau betrayed his intentions to kill Jacob in revenge for his plotting.

Fearing for Jacob's life, his mother Rebekah pleaded with Isaac to send Jacob to the land of his uncle, Laban. There he could both avoid Esau's wrath and finally find a wife from the same lineage as his parents. Agreeing with his wife's proposal, Isaac sent his son on his way with a final blessing.

Without so much as a camel to bear his belongings, Jacob departed both family and home, not knowing if he would ever return. He was currently only sixty miles into his five-hundred-mile journey. Having stopped each night to pitch camp, Jacob's progress was slow, much slower than initially expected. He was not an outdoorsy type like his brother but preferred to be in the tent of his parents, close to home. Every step he took was a step further from all he knew, but there was no going back.

Having figuratively hit rock bottom, Jacob ironically rested his head on a rock, unable to find a more suitable headrest. It would have to do. One would have thought that after seizing both his brother's birthright and blessing, Jacob would now be sleeping with the benefits afforded to him by these things. But, in his current moment of crisis, neither the blessing Jacob stole from Esau nor the one Isaac freely bestowed upon him offered Jacob any comfort. Instead, he dozed off to sleep in an unfamiliar land exposed to all the desert elements.

Jacob had alienated himself from everyone in his life, and in response, everyone (except his mother) had alienated themselves from him. That is why, when he laid his head down to sleep that night, he slept alone. No one was willing to undertake the journey with him, and no one cared enough for his plight to help him in his hour of greatest need. No wife, no children, no brother, no parents, and no friends – the stars were his only companions.

Certain Place

The Bible says that Jacob "reached a certain place..." (Gen. 28:11). Why does the Bible call it a "certain" place? Because even Jacob did not know where he was. The same is true for us. Many of us, right now, are in "certain" places. The only things certain about these "certain" places is uncertainty.

We do not know how long we will be there or how long before we will get out of there, but we remain stuck in a certain place in our journey called life oftentimes because of our own mistakes. Jacob had no one to blame but himself for his current misfortunes, but even in a "certain" place, God still sees. Even in an uncertain situation, God still moves.

The Setting Sun

Japan is notorious for its nickname as "the land of the rising sun," but more often than not, if we're honest, our lives resemble more of a setting sun than a rising sun. The Bible says that as Jacob came to that certain place, he "stopped for the night because the sun had set" (Gen. 28:11). The sun had set, and Jacob lacked any motivation to go further.

Likewise, some of us have experienced the sun set on our lives. When this happened, we lost all motivation to go further. We decided we would rather stay stuck in that "certain" place than press further into the unknown. Fortunately for Jacob, he only stayed one night in that certain place, in the land of the setting sun, but some of us have spent years in that place. Some of us have lost all hope that the sun will ever rise again, that it has set on our peace, on our joy, and on our hope, but what is shrouded in darkness, God is able to bring to light.

The Wilderness of Loneliness

We all, like Jacob, have been to the wilderness of isolation. If statistics prove anything, they all but unanimously agree that today's generation is the "loneliest" of any previous generations. Despite our technological advancements, we are more separated and lonelier than ever before.

A great number of people feel abandoned by culture, abandoned by man, and alone in a wilderness of uncertainty, not knowing what lies ahead or how far off they are from reaching their intended goal. In the same way, Jacob was only sixty miles into his journey. He still had to travel another treacherous 440 miles before he reached his uncle Laban's abode, but Jacob had never been that way before. He was daunted by the pressures of the wilderness and the pressures that accompanied loneliness.

So, what do you do when you are in a wilderness that you've never traversed and there is no one to guide or accompany you? What does man become when he is isolated from all else, cut off from the world and all his comforts? The answer—we become like Jacob. We wander. We wander towards a far-off place with only a glimmer of hope.

Yet, despite Jacob's poor circumstances and compromising personality, Jacob was about to become a product of God's blessing. Incredibly, God had big plans for Jacob. But Jacob first had to embrace the promise of God.

The Ladder to Heaven

Thus, while Jacob slept, the Bible says, "He had a dream in which he saw a stairway resting on the earth, with its top reaching to heaven, and the angels of God were ascending and descending on it" (Gen. 28:12).

God visited Jacob in a dream because sometimes the light shines the brightest when there is complete darkness. Yet, even when all hope seems lost, even when the end seems near, God is still working. The evening is darkest before the dawn.

It is after man reaches the end of his abilities that he truly understands the matchless ability of God. Thus, God proved that He could do more in Jacob's sleep than Jacob could do in his waking hours. And so, He gave Jacob a sneak peek into Heaven, the first human being to have been granted such a gift.

Notice, firstly, that the ladder's peak was in Heaven, but its foundation was on the Earth. The Bible consistently states that Earth is but God's footstool, an extension of His kingdom above. Thus, before God can show Jacob his purpose, He must first alter Jacob's perspective. God begins by showing Jacob his place in the order of things. In his position on the earth, Jacob stands at the bottom of the ladder, and this is where we all stand.

In the grand scheme of humanity, there is no hierarchy. We all live and die, we start at the bottom, and when all is said and done, we return to the bottom. Jacob, like all men, must learn his place before he can learn his purpose.

A Way Up and a Way Down

Surveying the ladder, Jacob noticed two things. He noticed firstly that there were angels *ascending* the ladder, and secondly, that there were angels *descending* the ladder. Thus, Jacob realized that the ladder was both a way up and a way down.

Never before had Jacob seen something so prodigious that he simply wanted to dart forward and race up the ladder. Yet, at the same time, Jacob also experienced a sense of dread, convicted of his inner sin and wickedness. He sensed that if he should even touch the ladder that was connected to something so otherworldly, he would surely die. He was not worthy to ascend the ladder. He was destined to die in shame and fear on the earth, separate from the Pure One who dwelt in unapproachable light.

Just when Jacob thought there was no hope, just when fear seemed to have the last word, Jacob's eyes latched onto a figure standing atop the staircase. It was God Himself, the doorway into Heaven, who alone judged who was worthy to ascend the ladder into Heaven. He did not hold a tribunal, nor did He delegate, but rather, He alone judged all matters. God was judge, jury, and executioner, and while Jacob saw this as a point of despair, it was, in fact, his only reason for hope. Jacob could never in his own power climb up the ladder, but God, in His endless mercy, purposed to climb down the ladder to save not only Jacob, but all those like him. Religion tells you to keep climbing. Religion tells you that you can make it on your own power, but grace does not make you climb the ladder.

Jacob's dream says nothing of him even attempting to climb the ladder, rather, grace says, "Don't even try! You'll never make it, but let me make the climb for you."

God Stands Above It

Notice God's position in Jacob's dream. "Then he dreamed, and behold, a ladder was set up on the earth, and its top reached to Heaven; and there the angels of God were ascending and descending on it. And behold, *the LORD stood above it*" (Gen. 28:13, NKJV) (emphasis added).

Think about the impact of these words. God stands above the stairway and everything beneath it. He stands above the whole universe! His physical location in Jacob's dream illustrates His sovereign position in relation to all else. He reigns above the schemes of man, the discord of the world, the hatred hurled at Him every minute of every day. He is triumphant over sin, death, and Satan. His thoughts and His ways are so much higher than ours (Is. 55:9). He alone is sovereign, which is especially comforting when we are in the wilderness of isolation, in the "certain" place of uncertainty.

Right now, in this age of global pandemics and racial tensions, it is important for humanity to realize that whatever plagues us, God stands above it. Whatever comes against us, God reigns above it. It might be stronger than us, it might be bigger than us, but my dad's bigger! My dad's stronger! He stands above pandemics and racial tensions, but He just doesn't stand above the big things. He also stands above those little things tucked away in your heart that you don't want anyone else to see. That is why before God can make you a promise, He must first give you a perspective.

He says, "I am, *El Shaddai*, God Almighty, and just as I visited Jacob in his dream, in his world of disruption and turmoil, so I will visit you in yours. Behold, no matter what trial or trouble you face, I stand above it!"[4]

God for Each One of Us

He said to Jacob, "I am the LORD, the God of your father Abraham and the God of Isaac" (Gen. 28:13).

Stirring in his slumber, Jacob vividly recalled the days of his youth when he and his brother Esau sat at his grandfather Abraham's feet. They listened to him recount the days long past when *El Shaddai* called him (then known as Abram) out of the land of Ur. *El Shaddai* promised him countless descendants, ironic since Abraham's only wife, Sarai (later Sarah) was old and barren. Nevertheless, God caused Sarah to conceive a son, Isaac, who in turn bore two sons, Esau and Jacob.

As a direct descendant of Abraham and Sarah, Jacob was a product of this miracle from *El Shaddai*. Indeed, if not for this miracle, he would not be living. Though Jacob did not yet know it, *El Shaddai* had a purpose for all Abraham's children, including Jacob.

Yet, what caused Jacob to frown in his sleep was not the fact that *El Shaddai* referred to Himself as the God of Abraham, but that He also referred to Himself as the God of Isaac, Jacob's father. This is the same father who overlooked Jacob throughout his life and who, by pushing his youngest son away, indirectly tempted Jacob to traverse down a path of lying and deception. It was as if his father had forgotten his most important purpose in life, to show his son how a servant of God was to act. Instead, Isaac left Jacob out of the picture, choosing instead to show favoritism to Esau. Thus, Jacob was disturbed to hear God refer to Himself as the God of Isaac.

You are the God of my father? Jacob thought. *If so, where were You when my father favored my brother over me? Where were You when my father ignored me and elevated another? If You are the God of my grandfather and my father, how come You were never the God for me?* These are thoughts that quite possibly infiltrated Jacob's mind, and, if we are being honest, similar thoughts seek to ensnare us. *You were there for my grandfather, God. You were there for my father. You blessed them, but I am alone. I'm far from home in this desert called life. I'm sleeping on a rock made of the unfortunate consequences of my choices. Why didn't You bless me like You blessed those before me? Are You not my God also?*

It is a human tendency to compare our poor circumstances with someone else's seemingly prosperous conditions and ask why does God bless some while seemingly overlook others.

Jesus answers this question at the end of His earthly ministry in John 21. In this passage, Jesus reveals that Peter will face a painful death in the near future. Immediately, Peter points his finger at John the Beloved, another of Christ's disciples. "Lord, what about him?" (John 21:21). Jesus answers Peter's question with a hint of frustration and chastisement. "If I want him to remain alive until I return, what is that to you? You must follow me" (John 21:21-22). These same words, Jesus echoes to each of us today. "Don't worry about how I bless him or her. Keep your eyes off others and their stuff. As for you, I know what you need. Keep your eyes on Me and follow Me."

Undeserved Blessings

And so, after revealing His identity, God declared to Jacob an astonishing promise.

> I will give you and your descendants the land on which you are lying. Your descendants will be like the dust of the earth, and you will spread out to the west and to the east, to the north and to the south. All peoples on earth will be blessed through you and your offspring.
>
> Genesis 28:13-14

Did I read that right? Jacob swindled his brother and tricked his father by snatching away his brother's birthright and blessing. Yet, instead of punishing Jacob more severely, instead of allowing Jacob to pay for his sins in full, God affirms the blessing! And what an astounding blessing it is!

God did not have to vindicate Isaac's blessing that Jacob stole from his brother. God is not bound to us simply because we infer His name. He could have justly told Jacob, "You wicked man, you have deceived your own family and have tried to come into the blessing prepared for the descendants of your grandfather Abraham, but I will withhold it from you. For none like you are deserving of such a blessing." God could have said this, and He would have been justified. He could have found another person to fulfill the promise to Abraham. He could have caused Rebekah to conceive in old age as He had Sarah do so, or even rejected Jacob and chosen to use Esau to fulfill His promise to Abraham and Isaac. Instead, God chose to bless Jacob abundantly according to His own will. Jacob received a very similar promise to that given to his grandfather and father, yet he would be the final patriarch. It was through his twelve sons that the tribes of Israel should come about.[5]

Even so, I look at this passage and admit, "Jacob would not have been my candidate. He's not trustworthy, rather he's immature, weak, and selfish. Surely, there must be someone else. But even if not, why bless this one wicked man just to fulfill a promise?"

How relieving that God does not operate according to human thinking. His thoughts are so much higher than ours, and *every* man He blesses is undeserving. We are all sinners in need of God's grace. Who are we to judge whom and how God blesses? Everything we have is a gift from God, even the breath in our lungs. While all of us have been abundantly blessed, the greatest blessing is not the material stuff. It is not the promise of future generations. In fact, God's greatest present to Jacob is the same one He promises to those who love His Name and long for His appearing: God Himself.

God's Presence—the Greatest Gift

God promised Jacob in verse 15, "I am with you and will watch over you wherever you go, and I will bring you back to this land. I will not leave you until I have done what I have promised you" (Gen. 28:15).

In other words, God told Jacob, "I was with your grandfather, I was with your father, and now I am with you. Behold, I will remain with you until the day you die." This is the greatest gift of all, for God to be with us. Thankfully, God promises that His presence will not be removed from His followers, but that He will always be with us.

The question is, do we live our lives in a consistent manner with this promise? Do we really believe that God is with us? Do we take heart in this promise? Do we even think of this as a blessing or do we just want the things He can give us? Do we think, *Aw, that's cool, God. I'm glad you're always with me, but if I'm being honest, it's not You I want. I just want your stuff.* It is a legitimate question: do we follow God for what He can give us or for who He is?

If we are in it for only the material blessings, most of us will be greatly disappointed. When God in the flesh lived on Earth among men, He did not live in a palace, He did not hire servants, He did not undertake one single thing to make His own life more comfortable. Nor did He provide His apostles with mansions or exquisite clothing or establish them as kings and emperors. On the contrary, though Jesus owned it all, He and His disciples lived in relative poverty, and nearly all of them died for their faith. Jesus came to free them from the shackles of self, not to enslave them all the more.

Jesus did not abuse His power, for His eyes were set not on Himself but on the things above, on the One who stands above it all. In the same manner, we should focus not on what we can get out of God in a materialistic sense but on what we can gain from Him in a mutual relationship. He has promised His presence, and that is above and beyond any gift we deserve.

Through You

So, why did God bless Jacob? Was it because God pitied Jacob? Was it because Jacob was deserving of such a blessing? By no means, rather, God blessed Jacob so that "All peoples on earth will be blessed through you and your offspring" (Gen. 28:14). Thus, it is not about what God can do *for* you, but what He can do *in* and *through* you. We are not blessed simply for our own benefit, but for the mutual benefit of others. The Gospel is not just a testimony of how I was blessed but also how I shared that same blessing with others.

Often in church today, we have developed this consumer mentality that God and the church should proctor to my needs, but have you ever imagined what God can accomplish through you if you allow Him to use you? The blessings that He gave you, that bonus from work, your abundance of clothes, that car you never use, He gave them to you so that you might be a blessing to others. Stop holding onto that which He gave you to release. Allow the investment God put in you to gain interest that the kingdom might prosper and the blessing of God spread to all nations, so that all might be blessed.

"Woke" Jacob

Following God's pronouncement of the blessing, the Bible says that "Jacob awoke from his sleep..." (Gen. 28:16). Jacob was the first "woke" person. He realized an important lesson, that if he should see God's promise come to fruition, he must wake up! He must arise from his slumber and move on from that "certain" place, from that lonely place, for he is not alone any longer.

Others in Jacob's culture would have told him that the "gods" only communicated with people at the people's homes, but God is not confined to "certain" places. Genesis 28 records Jacob going to sleep (Gen. 28:12) and waking from it (Gen. 28:16), but it never records God showing up. Rather, Jacob was the one who showed up. God was always there. This is His world; we are merely guests. That is why it is condescending to tell God at church, "God, we welcome your presence here."

"No," God says. "You've got it backwards. I welcome *your* presence here. This is my home." Should God be confined to "certain" places, He would be unable to visit us in our "certain" places. As it is, the limitless God cannot be put in a box, nor can His glory be contained. He sees all that is done on the Earth, and in His mercy and grace, He comes down to visit us in our "certain," lonely places.

Thus, in response to this incontrovertible fact, non-believers and believers alike ought to wake up. Wake up out of your slumber! Wake up out of the dream! Turn of the lullaby the world is singing you and see with fresh eyes the beauty of the dawn. Those who trust in Jesus will find that they, like Jacob, were once asleep in their sins. Yet, Jesus, with the simplest command, is able to arouse us from our sleep and invigorate us with new life and new perspective.

From Pillow to Pillar

The Bible says that "Early the next morning Jacob took the stone he had placed under his head and set it up as a pillar and poured oil on top of it" (Gen. 28:18). Jacob realized that the thing he was sleeping on was meant for a different purpose. It wasn't a pillow. It was a pillar. Jacob got it. His perspective was changed, and acknowledging his place in the order of things, he took that which he had formerly placed under him and set it over him.

Some of us need to learn this lesson, for if we are not careful, we treat God like Jacob did before he woke from his dream. God is said to be a Rock (Ps. 18:31), and a rock is not meant to be slept on. This would only provide discomfort, but this is what we do to God. We try to get Him to provide our comfort outside of His nature, but God is not the source of our comfort. Rather, He is the fount of our courage. He does not always provide us "comfort" in our "certain" place, but He always offers us courage. In order to access His courage, however, we have to stop using Him as a pillow, and start establishing Him in our life as the pillar He was always meant to be.

My Promise is My Pillow

God is not your pillow. He is your pillar. Do you know what your pillow is? Do you know what you *can* sleep on? If there is anything you can sleep on, sleep on God's promise. Sleep on it. God's promise is your pillow. How do I know this?

I know this because in Mark 4:35 the Bible says that "when evening had come, [Jesus] said to [His disciples], 'Let us go across to the other side.'" The disciples and Jesus were about to face the evening, just like Jacob did, and just like Jacob, the disciples sensed an overwhelming dread of alienation in that evening. A fierce squall tossed their rickety fishing boat like tumbleweed in the wind. Fearing for their lives, the disciples appealed to Jesus who was "asleep on a pillow" (Mark 4:38, NKJV). How could Jesus sleep in the midst of the storm? Jesus was able to sleep soundly because of the promise He made to His disciples that they would make it to the other side. He knew that He couldn't die in Mark 4 because He had a purpose to accomplish in Mark 5.

Know this, dear brother and dear sister, that the man and woman of God are invincible within the purpose and planning of God. The storms of life will come against you, but you can rest on His promise because you know, "I have a purpose on the other side, so it may look rough, but I'm going to make it to the other side, and my promise is my pillow!"

God is your pillar, the source of your courage, and His promise is the source of your comfort. So, when the storms of life come against you or when you are trapped in a "certain" place, you can sleep soundly on your pillow because your pillow is your promise.

This is the Gate!

Musing over his dream, Jacob remarked, "How awesome is this place! This is none other than the house of God, and this is the gate of heaven" (Gen. 28:17). What was a "certain" place, what was a wilderness, Jacob realized to be the gate of Heaven. Perspective requires patience to see things for what they really are. What you're going through may not look like it, but God declares over you, "This is the gate!" Your heartbreak…"this is the gate!" Your humbling…"this is the gate!" Your breaking is your breakthrough!

Given time, when God removes the scales from your eyes, and you receive this new perspective, you too will be able to say, "How awesome is this place?" That place of loneliness becomes the place of companionship. That "certain" place of uncertainty becomes the place of identity. This is the gate! So many people are sitting under this gate, they are sleeping under this gate. If only they would allow God to open their eyes, to give them a new perspective, that they might see the gate, which is the awesome provision of God in Christ Jesus our Lord.

Conclusion

Prior to Jacob's vision, Genesis records no account of another individual receiving a vision of God's blessed home. Jacob, therefore, was the first human being to see Heaven. This was curious, given Jacob's unruly nature.

By allowing Jacob to witness Heaven, God assured all future generations that -- despite mankind's sin, depravity, and wicked ways – hope remained. The God who stood above it all not only took notice of the righteous, but He also showed mercy to the unrighteous. In this manner, God illustrates that Heaven was not reserved for perfect beings, but it was accessible to all the redeemed.

Thus, one need not attempt to build a tower to Heaven to access God when God has already let down a ladder. There is no need to try to construct a way up when He has already brought that way down. While Jacob's vision was just that, a vision, it was a vision with real consequence.

A physical ladder stretching from Heaven to Earth does not exist by any means, but in the Gospel of John, when Jesus recruits the disciple Nathaniel, He makes known the interpretation of Jacob's vision. Jesus declares in John 1:51, "Very truly I tell you, you will see 'Heaven open, and the angels of God ascending and descending on' the Son of Man." Jesus was the one Jacob saw in his dream. It was Jesus, who descended Heaven's ladder in the form of a servant. He was the Way up to Heaven, promised in Genesis 28, and revealed in Matthew 1. To show humanity how to ascend, He had to descend. Thus, the way up came down.

VIII: MOSES, ON YOUR LEFT

Date: c. 1440 BC
Location: Sinai Peninsula

Little by little, Moses hewed away at the two slabs of stone with mixed feelings of anticipation and frustration. The two stone tablets Moses currently chiseled were meant to replace the two tablets delivered to Moses by God Himself, but which Moses had angrily broken.

Shaking his head, Moses remembered all too well that fateful day not long past when he had spoken with God atop Mount Sinai. True to His Word, God had brought His people out of the land of Egypt through mighty wonders, and true to his word, Moses had obediently directed God's people to Mount Sinai where God had promised to meet Moses again.

Giving specific instructions to Moses as to how the people were to conduct themselves when He descended, God had allowed the Israelites three days to prepare for His coming. Everyone was to be cleansed and was not to engage in any activity that might compromise cleanliness. Furthermore, anyone, be he human or animal, who approached the holy mountain and touched it would suffer instant death.

God had imposed these harsh preparational conditions on His people so that they might understand the seriousness of what it meant for God to "drop by" for a visit. This reminds me of when I was little, and my mom always instructed me to clean the house as if Jesus Himself were going to show up. While I am certain I never met the standard, that is exactly what the Israelites had to prepare for.

Sure enough, on the third day, Moses had gathered the people to meet God. Moses was like a man eager to introduce other individuals to a good friend of his. Staring with anticipation at the mountain, the Israelites had spied only the gathering of storm clouds. Nothing out of the ordinary. All of a sudden, the wind began to gust as the hairs on the back of their necks stood on end. Chills ran down their spines as even the most courageous among them trembled in fear.

Smoke clouded Mount Sinai denser than morning fog over a swamp, yet, where there is smoke, there is fire. Not long after the sight of smoke, God Himself descended in the form of blazing fire, akin to the flames first witnessed by Moses at the Burning Bush, where previously he had met God at this same mountain. Then, Moses caught only a glimpse of God's power, but when God descended in full sight of Israel, dread filled the people as they witnessed the very skies torn asunder by waves of flame.

The sign of fire was followed by fierce earthquakes as the presence of God alighted atop Mount Sinai. Trumpets signaled the arrival of the great King of kings, *Melech Malchei HaMelachim*, but above the trumpets could be heard the cry of Moses.

While before, when he first encountered the Living God, Moses had been unfamiliar with the great King of the universe, the same was no longer true. Moses had become acquainted with the inner nature and mind of God better than any other human being, even better than his great ancestor Adam. Unable to withhold the love he held towards his Maker and Sovereign, Moses cried aloud, and astonishingly, God answered Moses's cries.

Discerning Moses's voice above the thunder, above the earthquake, and above the sound of trumpets, God summoned Moses to join Him on the mountaintop. There, for forty days, Moses recorded the many laws of God, ten of which God Himself inscribed on two stone tablets. These were to be known as the Decalogue, or the Ten Commandments.

Before, God had allowed His miracles to be performed through objects such as Moses and Aaron's staff, but this was the first time Moses had held something that God Himself had specifically formed. Awed by the gesture, Moses carried the precious tablets down the mountain, only to find that in his time away, the Israelites had devolved into debauchery.

Rather than adhere to the promises of God, they doubted Moses and the will of God. Thus, they besought Aaron to make for them a god of their own liking in the form of a golden calf. Foolishly, Aaron acquiesced.

Speechless at this blatant act of rebellion, Moses was grieved to see the people turn away after their hour of deliverance. Nonetheless, he managed to intercede on the people's behalf before God and save them from destruction.

Even so, in the heat of his anger, Moses destroyed the Decalogue, God's Ten Commandments. Therefore, before the people could leave Sinai, the commandments had to be remade. For this purpose, God addressed Moses in Exodus 34.

A Personal Walk

God said to Moses:

> Chisel out two stone tablets like the first ones, and I will write on them the words that were on the first tablets, which you broke. Be ready in the morning, and then come up on Mount Sinai. Present yourself to me there on top of the mountain. No one is to come with you or be seen anywhere on the mountain; not even the flocks and herds may graze in front of the mountain.
>
> Exodus 34:1-3

Previously, Joshua had accompanied Moses up the mountain. This time, though, Moses must travel alone, with no one else to lean on, no one else to call to if trouble ensued. He was to entrust Himself entirely to God.

Similarly, this is how we are called to live out our faith. We cannot bring a Joshua alongside us in the hopes that, by his faith, we will be rescued. Rather, it is by God's grace that we are saved, and no one else's faith can save us. Yes, we are to walk alongside other believers; but, in the end, we are judged based solely on our own walk with God. Accordingly, God calls Moses to come up alone.

The God Who Came Down

In response to God's command, the text says, "So Moses chiseled out two stone tablets like the first ones and went up Mount Sinai early in the morning, as the Lord had commanded him; and he carried the two stone tablets in his hands" (Ex. 34:4). Moses approached his day obediently, bearing the tablets as he climbed the mountain. He was ready and willing to receive a word from God. Because of his obedience, God did something for Moses that He had never done before.

Previously, Moses had requested that God reveal Himself in all His glory. This is quite a request, yet God grants it. But He does so only in the way He sees fit, for no mortal can gaze upon God and live. Thus, as Moses ascends the mountain, the Bible says, "Then the Lord came down in the cloud and stood there with him and proclaimed his name, the Lord" (Ex. 34:5).

Moses could climb the mountain only so high. He could travel no further than the pinnacle; and, even if he were to reach the top, God would still be infinitely higher. This is how it is when mortals try to reach Heaven on their own terms. They soon discover that despite their abilities, despite their drive, they cannot and will not reach God without His aid. Looking down from Heaven, God sees Moses climbing the mountain. He watches as Moses stumbles and falls, as we all do in our spiritual walks, but in His grace, God descends from on high to meet with Moses. Moses could not get any higher, so God chose to come down.

But why should He? Why should God come down? *Moses should try harder*, we think. We convince ourselves that we need to do our best to get to God. The truth is, though, we cannot get to Him on our own. We need help.

The good news is that God is not sitting on His throne in Heaven, tapping His foot impatiently, and saying, "Come on, try harder! Stop being so faithless." God is a God of such humility that it pleases Him to come down from on high. He does not turn up His nose as He descends, thinking to Himself, "Why am I doing this? They should have to get to Heaven on their own." Instead, God lovingly comes down on His own accord and reveals Himself to His Creation.

The Revelation of Identity

Covered by the dust and dirt from his climb, Moses exhaled deeply as He watched God descend once more, but this time was different. His form was more glorious than ever, dazzling to Moses's eyes. Thus, before the light of God's *shekinah* glory could dissipate to a degree where Moses could perceive the form of Almighty God, God guided Moses towards a cleft in a nearby rock.

Moses felt the warmth of a hand on his shoulder, but he dared not turn around and disobey God's command, lest he risk death. His senses tingled with uncontrollable excitement and awe. He could not believe that God had acquiesced to his request!

At last, Moses perceived the appointed rock upon which God commanded him to stand. Tensing, Moses turned around anxious and expectant. Every second seemed like an eternity as he waited to see what all men desire, the form of the Creator. This was a moment Moses would never forget, a revelation unlike any given before his time.

After what seemed like forever, Moses spied a brilliant light approaching. Perceiving what appeared to be a hand falling over his face, Moses found his sight concealed but only for a moment.

When God removed His hand, Moses beheld the back of God, a wonder beyond all wonders. Astonished, Moses burst into tears, but God's divine revelation of His manifestation was not yet over. With a loud voice, He thundered in His passing,

The Lord, the Lord, the compassionate and gracious God, slow to anger, abounding in love and faithfulness, maintaining love to thousands, and forgiving wickedness, rebellion and sin. Yet he does not leave the guilty unpunished; he punishes the children and their children for the sin of the parents to the third and fourth generation.

Exodus 34:6-7

In His physical revelation, God also made known a divine revelation concerning His nature and His name. Names have meaning, and while people have often wondered how best to describe God, we need look no further than verses 6-7 to find ways God describes Himself. God does not conceal His identity, nor does He conceal His nature, but rather, He faithfully reveals Himself to those who earnestly seek Him.

A New Moses

Moses continued to lead the people of Israel for the duration of his life, until God Himself relieved Moses of his duties. Unfortunately, Moses rashly disobeyed God's explicit command, and being the just, impartial Judge, God refused to treat Moses any differently from the rest of the Israelites. Thus, because of his disobedience, Moses was forbidden to enter the Promised Land. Instead, he would hand over his role as Israel's leader to his successor, Joshua, and suffer the consequences of his actions.

It grieved Moses to know that he could not enter the Promised Land. This was the land that God had promised to Moses's forefathers, the patriarchs, and into which Moses had hoped to lead his people. Yet, as Moses wept bitterly, God sympathized with Moses's state, and, in His mercy, God allowed Moses to see the fruit of his labor.

Bidding his final farewells to his family, his friends, and his successor, Joshua, Moses ascended Mount Nebo in the presence of God. God had guided his steps from the day of his birth; thus, it was fitting that God would act as his tour guide to the Promised Land. Moses would be the first of all the Israelites to behold the land flowing with milk and honey which God had prepared for His people.

Moses trudged up the mountain eager at last to behold the long-awaited destination. He had heard rumors of this land ever since he was a child, and now at last, he would behold it with his own eyes. Upon reaching the top of the mountain, Moses sensed the immediate presence of God.

Long had God waited to pull the curtain and reveal the Promised Land. Now, it was finally time. Speaking directly to Moses, God said, "This is the land I promised on oath to Abraham, Isaac and Jacob when I said, 'I will give it to your descendants.' I have let you see it with your eyes, but you will not cross over into it" (Deut. 34:4).

Tears welled up in Moses's eyes as he breathed a sigh of relief and nodded his head. The land was good. It was very good. It reflected the beauty of the infant days of Earth when God created the world in all its splendor and wonder. Surely, the Promised Land was worth the wait.

Moses had seen God, and now he had seen the land of God's promise. Thus, at one hundred twenty years old, with life still left in him, Moses knew that his time on Earth had come to an end. He had served faithfully for forty years as God's prophet and Israel's leader, and his work was now complete.

Slumping forward, Moses's body ceased to operate, his heart silent within his chest. Yet, rather than have his body unceremoniously left for the scavengers, Moses was given one last honor in death.

A brilliant light encompassed Moses once more as God came down from Heaven for the purpose of burying one of His servants. God could have assigned this task to an angel, or He could have merely gestured with His finger and consigned Moses to a place of burial. But He attended to Moses's body personally. Moses was a true friend of God, and thus, God treated him as such.

With His own hands, God buried Moses, covering with dirt one descended from dirt. Moses's body had returned to the ground from which all men originated, but Moses's story did not end there.

Sure enough, centuries later when Jesus with His apostles, Peter, James, and John, ascended the Mount of Transfiguration, and He was transformed in their sight, He was visited by two individuals. One of them was the renowned prophet Elijah, and the other was none other than Moses himself. At long last, Moses had entered the Promised Land.

Conclusion

Of all the prophets of God, none was more familiar with the mind of God than Moses. The Bible states that "The Lord would speak to Moses face to face, as a man speaks with his friend" (Ex. 33:11). Indeed, God even granted Moses's request to see His glory.

In the context of this intimate relationship, God disclosed to Moses certain mysteries previously concealed. For instance, one may reasonably assume that, by way of revelation, God identified "Jesus" as the name of God's Son and the Savior of the world. God also revealed the title of "Messiah," referring to God's Anointed One. The reason for this assumption is that, unable to contain his joy, Moses renamed his successor "Hoshea" to "Joshua," which is Hebrew for "Jesus." Additionally, he bestowed upon his brother Aaron the title of "High Priest," which in Hebrew is *mashiach*, translated "messiah." In these ways, Moses indicated that the Creator of the universe who made Himself known to Moses would later reveal Himself to all men as "Jesus, the Messiah," so that all might know Him as Moses did.

When God revealed His glory to Moses, God foreshadowed the day when He would come down on His own accord, and His glory, the glory of the one and only Son, would become flesh and make His dwelling among us. By so doing, God would reveal His glory to all, not just to Moses. As Timothy Keller put it in his book *Prodigal Prophet*: "Only when you look into the gospel of Jesus Christ does all the goodness of God pass before you, and it's not the back parts anymore.... There's the glory of God in the face of Christ through the gospel." Praise God that the way up brought His glory down!

IX: GHOSTED

Date: 592 BC
Location: Solomon's Temple

Ezekiel burst into tears, his hand concealing his creased forehead. He had just witnessed the most horrific vision conveyed to one of God's prophets: that of God abandoning His people. Ezekiel had grown accustomed to completing odd assignments for God, such as lying on his side for 390 days to fulfill a symbolic action, or eating food cooked over dung. Nevertheless, such deeds paled in comparison to the alarming thought of God leaving the Temple. What grieved Ezekiel even more so was that the Jewish people had grown so stubborn in their wickedness that they did not even recognize the absence of God.

They had become, once more, like the people of Babel. Contriving a god of their own design, the Jewish people no longer acknowledged the presence of God. For this reason, God removed Himself from their midst and from His holy Temple.

The Tabernacle

The Temple was the center of Jewish faith for thousands of years, owing to long historical tradition. Upon the very mount that the Temple was erected, God tested Abraham's faith by calling on him to sacrifice his son, Isaac. Perceiving Abraham's faith and obedience, God stayed Abraham's hand. Notably, in this same passage, Genesis 22, the word "worship" is first used. This is no mere coincidence, for the mount upon which Abraham nearly sacrificed his son would later become the central location for Israelite worship and sacrifice.

Yet, before the Israelites worshipped and sacrificed to God in the Temple, in the days of Moses God dwelled among His people in the Tent of Meeting (also known as the Tabernacle). This portable tent suited the Israelites' nomadic lifestyle during their wilderness journey, as it could be taken down and again erected whenever and wherever the people pitched camp. Its portability did not diminish its sacredness, though. God provided Moses strict instructions concerning the tent's purpose and design. Moses followed God's directives to the letter, setting the tent up outside the Israelite camp.

In accordance with God's command, the Israelites prayed in the direction of the tent, acknowledging that the presence of God was in their midst. They were careful to obey all God's decrees, keeping appropriate distance from the tent and the holy of holies, into which God allowed only the high priest to enter. This portable tent was richly furnished and stood more than fifteen feet tall as a way of impressing upon the Israelites the enormity of God. The time eventually arrived when the Israelites would no longer wander aimlessly, however, at which point God would voice His desire for a temple.

David's Dilemma

After their wilderness wanderings, God had delivered His people into the Promised Land and eventually established, at their request, an earthly kingship. King Saul, Israel's first king, proved incapable of leading God's people, so God appointed a young shepherd boy named David to succeed him. A fierce warrior and devoted worshipper of God, David and his mighty men won battle after battle. Upon conquering Jerusalem, King David established an altar in the midst of the city with the intention of making Jerusalem both the political and religious center of his kingdom. When David conceived to construct a temple, though, God spoke to him and revealed that David had shed too much blood to build God's house. God needed a pure man, someone whose hands were not covered in blood, to build His Temple. For this purpose, David enlisted his son, Solomon, to inherit his dream.

Sometimes this is the case in our own lives where we have a genuine desire to serve God in some capacity, and yet He reveals to us that His desire is to use another for that goal. In my own life, I remember last year when my dad and I were having a heart-to-heart conversation as we strolled along the beach, and he told me something I never knew. He said that ever since he had gotten saved, he dreamed of being a pastor. He wanted to serve God from the pulpit, but he said it had become clear to him over time that God had assigned this task to another individual close to my father: me.

Both David and my dad had good intentions, but God, for reasons of His own, seems to have chosen to use someone else to fill certain roles. Simply because God selected someone other than David to build the Temple, however, did not keep David from doing everything he could to help his son in the process. In fact, before Solomon even knew about his monumental task, David had already furnished a stockpile of the necessary items for the Temple's construction. In the same way, over the years, my father, whether or not he knows it, has prepared me for full-time ministry. By setting forth a godly example, by discipling me during weekly lunches, and by spending time with me, my father has helped mold me into the man I have become.

Thus, we can take comfort in that, while God may desire to use another individual for the purpose we had in mind, He can still use us to aid that person in the process—all for His glory.

Temple Construction

When Solomon built the Temple, religious sacred centers of worship dotted the known world. Yet, Solomon's Temple would surpass all of them in wonder and splendor. The ground laid aside for the Temple was so revered by Solomon and all of Israel that not a stone was fashioned on that spot. Rather, Solomon had his workers complete work on each stone at the quarry before delivering them to the Temple site. Thus, from the outset, Solomon established the solemn reverence that was to be shown concerning the Temple ground.

Solomon spent seven years constructing the Temple, by which time it was a wonder of the world. Modern estimates approximate the Temple's cost in today's monetary terms to be nearly eighty-seven billion dollars! To put this in perspective, the most lavish private residence in the world today, Buckingham Palace, is roughly estimated at only between two and five billion. Solomon's Temple, on the other hand, surpassed all temples built before it, so that on the day he dedicated the building to God, Solomon was greatly pleased with his work.

Temple Dedication

Offering a humble prayer at the Temple's dedication, Solomon waited with all the elders of Israel for God to make good on His promise to David. Would the God of Heaven truly dwell in a house made by the hands of men?

Even Solomon had his doubts. When uttering his prayer, he voiced his concerns asking, "But will God really dwell on earth with humans? The heavens, even the highest heavens, cannot contain you. How much less this temple I have built!" (2 Chron. 6:18).

Later prophets, such as Isaiah, would question how any man could build an abode worthy of God's presence. Anything we give Him, anything we do for Him, no matter how magnificent, ultimately falls immensely short of His standard. As the Almighty God, it is His prerogative to set the standard. And His standard is absolute perfection. Unfortunately, none of us meet that impossible standard. Therefore, we can easily fall into a cycle of depression where we think we can never please God. But God, in His infinite mercy, accepts our imperfect gift out of the love He has for us.

It is like a young boy who told his father that he had bought his dad a gift. Surprised, the father asked to see it. Withdrawing his hand from behind his back, the boy proudly revealed a tacky yellow tie, depicting a hula dancer and the word "Aloha" lit up with red and green lights. Upon receiving his son's gift, the father thanked his son, though inwardly thinking to himself that he would simply stash the tie away with the other gifts he never used. The next day, however, as the man was preparing to leave to give an important business presentation, his son approached him, tie in hand. He begged his father to wear it, deeming it perfect for this special day. The father acquiesced and exchanged his designer silk tie for his son's tacky yellow one – not because of the tie's sudden attractiveness, but because of the father's love for his child.

Like the boy's father, God shows us the same love such that instead of disregarding our gift, He accepts our prayers, showing us His loving kindness. Thus, "When Solomon finished praying, fire came down from heaven and consumed the burnt offering and the sacrifices, and the glory of the LORD filled the temple" (2 Chron. 7:1). God was pleased to come down.

Solomon and those with him fell prostrate and immediately worshipped God, praising Him for hearing their prayers. The King of Heaven had come down to dwell in the midst of the people of Earth.

A Shell of Purpose

If only the people had been persistent in their unadulterated worship at the Temple! Unfortunately, they did not. Instead, they violated the stipulations God had clearly established. Upon the Israelites' repeated, persistent disobedience and desecration of the Temple, God refused to dwell in the midst of idolatrous people any longer. Thus, one day, He essentially packed up and left. God allowed the prophet Ezekiel to witness His departure. Ezekiel described how "The glory of the Lord went up from within the city and stopped above the mountain east of it" (Ez. 11:23). God relocated Himself to the

Mount of Olives, outside the city limits, as a means of fore-shadowing His future plans.

He is a patient God, and a merciful one, but the priests and all Israel had abused His patience. God would not be mocked. His presence was manifest in the Garden, and men rejected Him. He then manifested His presence in what was supposed to be a sacred temple, and yet, again, men rejected Him. Thus, God completely removed His presence from the Temple so that it remained an empty building. It was only a shell of its purpose.

This is how many of us live our lives apart from God. God has a unique purpose for each of us. When we malign His intent, though, we desecrate our purpose. Oh, how it would be far better for us to submit to God's will that we might receive the blessing of His presence!

I'll be Back

Even with His departure, God did not leave Ezekiel in utter hopelessness. Rather, He promised Ezekiel that the day would come when God's glory would return to the land of Israel, and He would live among His people once more. During this time, there would be a new temple, far more glorious than that of Solomon. And from the same place that God's glory departed the Temple, that of the east gate, God would return.

In partial fulfillment of God's promise, the Israelites were permitted by the Persian ruler to return to their land. There, under the guidance of Ezra and Nehemiah, the Israelites rebuilt the Temple, which the Babylonians had previously destroyed. Even so, the Scriptures take care to note that God's glory did not visibly return to the Temple. The Israelites, like their ancestors, failed to realize that the Temple was only the dwelling place of God. It was not inherently sacred, rather, God's Spirit made it sacred.

Thus, for the next four hundred years, the Israelites performed sacrifices and worshipped God in the Temple, hoping that one day God's glory might return in fulfillment of His promise and that He might dwell once again with people. During that time, they were subjected under the Persians, Greeks, Hasmoneans, and Romans, all of whom mocked the Jews for their faith. Yet, in the fullness of time (Gal. 4:4), God was to keep His promise with Israel. His glory would return to the Temple, and His presence would dwell among the Israelites, but not in the way they had expected. The Israelites would discover that they were quite unaware of God's true intentions.

God's Plan

Often, we seek to formulate God's promise into that which we think benefits us the most. For example, when we read in the Bible where God says, "'For I know the plans I have for you,' says the Lord, 'plans to prosper you and not to harm you'" (Jer. 29:11), we frequently assume that His plans are the same as our own desires because, we reason, how better to prosper us? In focusing on our own dreams, though, we might overlook the import of this verse, which is that *God* has a plan. The goal of His plan is found in the following verses: "Then you will call on me and come and pray to me, and I will listen to you. You will seek me and find me when you seek me with all your heart" (Jer. 29:12). His plan is that we seek Him and find Him, not that He gives us whatever we want.

Many of us may not like the latter verses, because truthfully, we are not really interested in finding Him. We want instead to be able to direct God's plan to match our plan. Thus, the question is: Do we trust God even when we may not prefer or do not even know His plan? God may not do everything we want or reveal every detail to us, but He promised that in all things, He "works for the good of those who love him, who have been called according to his purpose" (Rom. 8:28). If God has called you, then this means that He has a purpose for you, and that purpose is good! It may be difficult to trust God when you do not agree with him or understand His plan, but this is where faith comes in. Faith is the assurance of things hoped for. We cannot always foresee God's exact plan, but we trust in God, knowing that He is for us and not against us (Rom. 8:31), and that He is faithful to do what He has promised. He will reveal His plan to each of us at the proper time, just as He did to the awaiting Israelites.

Thus, for four hundred years the Jews waited, longing for God's glory to return to the Temple, for Him to dwell among people once more. Yet, in the fullness of time (Gal. 4:4), God was to keep His promise with Israel. His glory would return to the Temple, and His presence would dwell among the Israelites, but not in the way they had expected.

Teenage Jesus

Downcast, Mary and Joseph entered the Temple courts to pray and seek God's favor. For the last three days, they searched Jerusalem frantically for their lost son. Jesus was never one to cause trouble, but this Passover was different. Both Mary and Joseph thought when they had left Jerusalem that Jesus was with His friends and relatives; but when they searched for Him, they could not find Him.

Fear clutched their hearts as they pondered the fate that might have befallen their son. Had they carelessly left Him behind in the city, or had He lost His way along the road back home? Passover attracted people from far and wide. Who knows what people Jesus might come across? Male children like Him made prospect slaves, or worse.

Terrified, Mary and Joseph returned to Jerusalem, where they searched for Jesus for three days. With no luck, they entered the Temple courts to pray. Perhaps God might aid them in their quest and unite them once more with their son. Sure enough, no sooner had the couple entered the Temple courts than they found a sight that astonished them.

Their twelve-year-old son was sitting among the teachers of the law, engaged in deep theological discourse. Not only did He listen carefully to the words spoken by the rabbis, but He also questioned them and answered them with wisdom that astounded all. Even so, Jesus' parents scolded Him for the scare He had given them. Mary asked Him, "Son, why have you treated us like this? Your father and I have been anxiously searching for you" (Luke 2:48).

"Why were you searching for me?" he asked. "Didn't you know I had to be in my Father's house?"

Neither Joseph nor Mary understood what Jesus was saying, and rather than press Him further, they led Jesus back home, making Him promise to never scare them like that again. In compliance with His parents' wishes, Jesus was obedient to them, and He "grew in wisdom and stature, and in favor with God and man" (Luke 2:52).

New Temple

Little did the teachers know that day that the boy with whom they were speaking was the answer to the prayers Israelites had been praying for centuries. God had heard their cry, and He sent His own Son, the temple made of flesh, for the salvation of all.

From His youth, Jesus possessed a certain affinity for the Temple in Jerusalem, but upon His return to the Temple in later years, Jesus revealed that the temple of His body far surpassed the worth of the Temple of stone. While the stone Temple was carved by human hands, Jesus' human form was the work of the Holy Spirit (Luke 1:35). While innumerable sacrifices were performed in the stone Temple to pardon sin till the next offense, Jesus made a radical promise. He stated that should the temple of His body be laid to rest for three days; He would pardon sin permanently for all those who believed in Him (John 2:19).

This new temple, the temple of His body, was the incarnation of God's presence. The story of His divine presence had reached its climatic chapter: The Garden of Eden was established by it; Mount Sinai reintroduced it; the Tabernacle and Temple were the loci of it. Now, Jesus was the personification of it. No longer did men need to travel to a stone building to seek forgiveness of sins. Rather, the better Temple had come to men: all those who put their faith in Jesus would be cleansed of all unrighteousness, and they would see the glory of God, just as He promised. The Way up had now come down in the flesh.

Conclusion

Have you ever been ghosted before? Or maybe you were the one who did the ghosting? In either case, you know the feeling of either receiving silence from another individual or providing silence to someone else.

Sometimes, this is our view of God, and this was most certainly the view of the Israelites. For four hundred years, God was silent. No prophets, no new Scriptures, no signs, nothing. By all standards, it seemed that God had ghosted the Israelites. At the hour when they least expected it, though, God showed up.

In the words of Gandalf from *The Lord of the Rings*, "A wizard is never late...Nor is he early. He arrives precisely when he means to." While God is certainly no wizard, the same can be said for Him. God is never late. Nor is He early. He arrives exactly when He means to, in the fullness of time; and, when He does, He fulfills His promise to the letter. The Israelites were looking forward to a new temple made of stone where God would dwell, but God gave them something much better: His own Son in human flesh.

For thousands of years, Jews and Gentiles alike wondered how they might reach Heaven. Was it through constructing a tower, ascending a staircase, offering sacrifices, obeying laws? In the end, all their efforts were in vain. No matter what they did, Heaven continued to remain out of their reach. Humanity could never reach Heaven. Like Aesop's fox and the grapes, Heaven would always loom too high and unattainable.

Instead of scoffing at humanity, however, Heaven provided an alternative. If humanity could not reach Heaven, Heaven would stoop down and pull humanity up. Yes, this was the only way that Heaven could ever be truly obtained, by wrapping Himself in human flesh and personally coming down to humanity.

PART THREE

Road Narrows: The Only Way

X: BACK TO THE WOMB

Date: c. AD 27
Location: Jerusalem

Passover season for Jews is the busiest time of year. Pilgrims from the four corners of the earth gather in Jerusalem in accordance with the Law of Moses to remember God's faithfulness. In years past, the Jewish people were enslaved under the tyrannical rule of the Egyptian Pharaohs, but, through Moses, God freed them from bondage.

To set the Israelites free, however, God sent a death angel to strike the land of Egypt, killing every firstborn son. At God's command, Moses instructed his fellow Israelites to mark the doorposts of their homes with lamb's blood so that the angel of death might "pass over" them. It was after this fateful day that the Israelites were finally released from Egyptian slavery. To commemorate His freeing them from bondage, God directed the Israelites to celebrate Passover as a holy day of remembrance. Accordingly, the Israelites annually celebrated the national holiday of Passover, reminding themselves of God's deliverance.

Ironically, while Israelites from the global community packed the inns and homes of Jerusalem, they could not help but notice the large Roman presence in the Holy City. Over time, the Israelites' oppressors had simply replaced one for another. Before, it was the Pharaoh of Egypt. Now, it was the Caesar of Rome. Even so, there were whispers amongst the Jewish community of the coming Messiah, one who, like Moses, would set the people free from the tyranny of Rome. However, with all the talk of the Messiah, people began to forget the promise God made through Moses of a prophet greater than he. Moses was the most revered of all Israelites. None were considered to be in as favorable light with God as he who saw God face to face; but Moses himself said that "The Lord your God will raise up for you a prophet like me from among you, from your fellow Israelites. You must listen to him" (Deut. 18:15).

While most Jews overlooked this promise of a prophet in hope of the promise of a protector, men such as Nicodemus tended to balance both in the hopes of having a clearer understanding of God's will. The wise Nicodemus was often viewed by his fellow peers and others alike as a righteous man, one endowed by the wisdom and compassion of the Most High.

Nicodemus was one of only seventy-one privileged Jews to sit on the Great Sanhedrin, the supreme legislative and judicial branch of Judea. While Rome held the ultimate power in the land, the Great Sanhedrin acted within its parameters, overseeing Jewish religious and ceremonial laws and traditions. The Great Sanhedrin wielded significant influence throughout

Judea, and Nicodemus was honored to be numbered amongst the select few on this prestigious court.

Over the years, he had risen from a pupil, to a Phariseetical rabbi, to now a "teacher of teachers." As such, Nicodemus had both taught and learned from a large number of Jewish rabbis, all of them different in their own right, but none of them truly standing apart from the others.

All this changed one day when Nicodemus either received word, or was present, when a man called Jesus overturned the tables of the moneychangers and moneylenders at the Temple. Becoming indignant with the exploitative tradesmen, Jesus used a makeshift whip to drive sacrificial lambs and animals from the temple courts. This incensed a number of the teachers of the law, who accused Jesus of disrupting the festivities of Passover, the largest Jewish holiday of the year. But Jesus seemed to have no qualms with causing a scene.

Shockingly enough, when some of Nicodemus's colleagues demanded Jesus show them a sign to support His authority to commit such a brazen act, Jesus answered, "Destroy this temple, and I will raise it again in three days" (John 2:19).

The Jewish leaders marveled at Jesus' claim, knowing that the temple construction took forty-six years, but many in Jerusalem at Passover believed in Jesus and His signs. Therefore, the Jewish leaders began to conspire against Jesus, hoping to trap Him in His own words. Doubtless, they plotted how they might snare Him, but Nicodemus's interest was piqued. Jesus was unlike the rabbis Nicodemus was accustomed to hearing, for He spoke as one with authority. Thus, determined to hear Jesus' side of the story for himself, Nicodemus hastily sent word to Jesus to set up a meeting between the two, rabbi to rabbi.

Jesus was young in years, reckless by Nicodemus's standards, but the older Jewish leader hoped to straighten out the rogue Nazarene. Perhaps, through wise counsel, Nicodemus could discern Jesus' true motives and pass on years of experiential wisdom. At the same time, Nicodemus hoped to learn more concerning Jesus' message. Jesus' words challenged the rabbi's rigid thinking. Intrigued and longing to know more, Nicodemus "came to Jesus at night" (John 3:2).

Status vs Solution

While Nicodemus desired to learn further from Jesus, he hoped to do so on his own terms. Jesus must meet Nicodemus at the time and place appropriate for Nicodemus's purposes. In the daylight hours, Nicodemus was preoccupied with serious matters and could not be interrupted by Jesus' agenda. Furthermore, if Nicodemus was to approach Jesus in broad daylight, rumors might circulate that he was a Jesus sympathizer. Nicodemus wanted answers, but not at the expense of his social status. Thus, to defuse suspicion, Nicodemus took precautions.

Such terms and disrespect would have surely deterred a number of rabbis from meeting with Nicodemus, but Jesus was not daunted by Nicodemus's lack of faith or by his social standing. Characteristic of Jesus, He graciously and wisely met the level of faith of His listener. So, despite Nicodemus's reservations and precautions, Jesus decided to hear him out when he came calling.

If only more Christians were like Jesus. Unfortunately, because of animosity, many Christians are not willing to engage in amicable conversations with people of opposing viewpoints. Creationists refuse to meet with naturalists and apologists ignore the invitations of philosophers. But Jesus set aside His cultural and theological differences to meet with someone who did not see eye to eye with Him. Why? Because Jesus cared about the individual. For this reason, He made the necessary accommodations that night, such that when Nicodemus arrived, Jesus sat down at the table with Him and said, "Let's talk! What is it you want to know?"

Help Me with My Unbelief

Jesus' treatment of Nicodemus is revolutionary compared to what many evangelists teach today. Word of Faith theologians assert that unless you have sufficient faith, God will overlook your plea. Twisting Scripture to conform to their agenda, these false teachers assert that if you can name it, then God will claim it for you. If you cannot name it, though, because your faith is not strong enough, you will be unable to claim it.

This may seem like good news to some, but for many who are honest, they do not have the prescribed faith to achieve such feats. Rather, they are like the father in Mark 9, who brings his demon-possessed son to Jesus. The father begs Jesus to cast the demon from his son saying, "But if you can do anything, take pity on us and help us" (Mark 9:22).

"'If you can'?" said Jesus. "Everything is possible for one who believes" (Mark 9:23).

Some people erroneously view Jesus as a smug or condescending, merciless man, with arms crossed and nose raised, as if He would refuse to look upon the unbelief of others. As if it were beneath Him. This is not, however, the Jesus we see presented in Mark 9.

Rather, upon Jesus' words, the father exclaimed emphatically, "I do believe; help me overcome my unbelief!" (Mark 9:24-25). Did Jesus reject the father for his unbelief? Did he tell him, "Too bad. Better luck next time"? No. What Jesus did was grant the man's request: he rebuked the impure spirit. "'You deaf and mute spirit,' he said, 'I command you, come out of him and never enter him again'" (Mark 9:25).

In this account, Jesus illustrates that He willingly aids those who admit their lack of faith. What a relief! There are times in my own life when I confess to God that my faith is weak. If the Word of Faith preachers are right in assuming that God will ignore me for such a confession, I have no hope. However, Jesus condescended to the level of the boy's father, just as He condescended to the level of Nicodemus's faith. He does not wait for us to procure the necessary level of faith before taking interest in our lives. Rather, He takes our unbelief upon Himself and offers us a new perspective, that we might see the light of His truth and our faith would increase.

Sent by God

Coming face to face with Jesus, Nicodemus begins by saying, "Rabbi, we know that you are a teacher who has come from God. For no one could perform the signs you are doing if God were not with him" (John 3:2).

While many of the Pharisees considered Jesus to be demon-possessed or even a Samaritan, Nicodemus was quick to acknowledge both Jesus' skill and anointing as a rabbinical teacher. It is one thing for Nicodemus to say that Jesus is a good teacher, but it is another for him to say that God has appointed Jesus as a teacher. How did Nicodemus know this? Why was he convinced?

Nicodemus offers the answer for his belief at the end of verse 2: "For no one could perform the signs you are doing if God were not with him."

While other Jewish teachers of the law associated Jesus' miracles with demonic power, Nicodemus recognized that such supernatural acts could be performed only in accordance with God's will. This being the case, Jesus of Nazareth was different. He was not just a good teacher; He was someone sent by God. But for what purpose and to what end?

Born Again

Jesus answered, "Very truly I tell you, no one can see the kingdom of God unless they are born again" (John 3:3).

Jesus' off-the-cuff retort may, on surface level, seem snarky and dismissive, but the Bible says that Jesus "answered" Nicodemus. What had He answered? Nicodemus made a statement, not a question, but the omniscient Jesus perceived Nicodemus's mind, discerning the question behind his words. Jesus did not waste time on idle conversations. As in most cases in the Bible, He shot straight to the point. Rather than thanking Nicodemus for His compliment or confirming Nicodemus's claim, Jesus instead dove into the plan for salvation: it is necessary for an individual to be born again if He is to be saved.

"'How can someone be born when they are old?' Nicodemus asked. 'Surely they cannot enter a second time into their mother's womb to be born!'" (John 3:4).

Oftentimes in rabbinic conversation, an individual would attempt to ask questions to a rabbi to flesh out an answer.

Nicodemus was aware of how preposterous it would be for an individual to re-enter his mother and be physically born again, so in posing the question, he hoped Jesus might provide an alternative solution. Sure enough, Jesus came prepared.

The Two Births

Jesus answered, "Very truly I tell you, no one can enter the kingdom of God unless they are born of water and the Spirit. Flesh gives birth to flesh, but the Spirit gives birth to spirit" (John 3:5-6).

It is no coincidence that Jesus used "birth" to refer to the conversion of believers. Following conception, a mother gives birth, and in a similar way, Christian converts are first conceived before they are born. This conception comes through the process whereby God calls people unto Himself. Following conception, men and women are born through regeneration by the Spirit. Just as the child had nothing to do with his physical birth, so the believer has nothing to do with his spiritual birth. It is a work wholly of God (Eph. 2:8-9). Birth cannot be contributed to. It can only be received. Likewise, Jesus illustrates to Nicodemus that we cannot contribute to our own spiritual birth. We can only receive it.

Curiously, evangelists over the years have been calling on people to be born again. "Say this prayer!" "Follow these steps!" "Read this book if you want to be born again!" In so doing, these evangelists miss the whole point. The very concept of rebirth is alien to human understanding. Jesus is calling for a complete reset. Only by beginning over can we truly progress.

Born of the Flesh

Culturally, Nicodemus understood the significance of birth. He was born a Jew, and many Jews during Nicodemus's time believed that one's blood heritage secured their salvation. Jews, like Nicodemus, loved to quote Deuteronomy 7:6 which says, regarding the Jewish nation, "For you are a people holy to the LORD your God. The LORD your God has chosen you out of all the peoples on the face of the earth to be his people, his treasured possession." However, they choose to selectively overlook verse 7 which says, "The Lord did not set His love on you nor choose you because you were more in number than any other people, for you were the least of all peoples."

God did not choose the nation of Israel because He was awed by their splendor. Rather, He identifies their meekness, through which His glory will be better perceived. The emphasis was on God's covenant with the patriarchs, a covenant to display His glory; but many of the Israelites, and later Jews, applied the covenant according to their own theology. Rabbis taught that only Jews could be saved due to God's covenant with Israel, thus, for a Gentile to be saved, he had to be converted.

Jews believed that there were necessary steps by which Gentiles, such as Rahab and Ruth, could become Jews. Yet, Jesus made no indication to Nicodemus that the rebirth He spoke of was one that could be obtained through human performance. Rather, it was a work only God could achieve.

To this end, Jesus utterly rejected the notion that salvation was reserved only for the Jewish nation, even teaching a parable wherein a Jewish man was sentenced to Hades (Luke 16:24). Both He, and John the Baptist, affirmed that God could make children of Abraham from the stones of the ground (Luke 3:8), and thus, true salvation came not from one's physical birth but from one's spiritual rebirth.

Spiritual Rebirth

Notice that Jesus said that one must be born "again." This being the case, Jesus acknowledges that Nicodemus and others have already been born, and when they were born, they possessed a sin nature. When Adam sinned, his sin nature was inherited by his descendants, and thus, it was necessary for an individual to be reborn to enter the kingdom of God. Thus, that individual must die.

What Jesus promised following that spiritual death is the act of regeneration. Regeneration is to the soul what resurrection is to the body. To enter the kingdom of God, believers require a new nature (2 Cor. 5:17). Their old nature is incapable of understanding the ways of God or of growing closer to Him. Thus, believers must receive the new nature that can come only through the work of the Holy Spirit.

To employ an analogy, dogs cannot comprehend the philosophy of Aristotle. Dogs are incapable of grasping such lofty things. What they need is not more hours of lectures, but rather, they need a completely different nature, a human nature, to enable them to understand. The same is true for us. What we need is not another crash course in philosophy, but the regenerative work of the Holy Spirit, so that we might have a new nature that will allow us to better understand God and have a relationship with Him.

The Gospel in a Nutshell

Driving His point home concerning the inclusivity of salvation, Jesus delivers the most well-known verse in Scripture.

Often referred to as "the Gospel in a nutshell," John 3:16 includes twenty-six words. These twenty-six words sum up the entirety of Scripture in such a beautiful way that, while John 3:16 is often the most overused Bible verse, it is also the most inexplicable verse.

Jesus tells Nicodemus, "For God so loved the world that he gave his one and only Son, that whoever believes in him shall not perish but have eternal life" (John 3:16).

For God *so loved.* Jesus does not say that God "so hated" the world or that He "so resented" it. Nor does Jesus proclaim that God "kind of cared for" the world. Rather, God "so loved" the world with a love beyond human understanding.

For God so loved *the world.* Jesus does not say, "God so loved the Jews," or, "God so loved the Greeks," but rather He claimed that God loved the world as a whole. The Jews of that day and age were particularly nationalistic and firmly believed that they were God's chosen people. They even attempted to stone Jesus on one occasion for inferring that God's presence might be turned towards the Gentiles. Such was the extent of their disdain for Gentiles that they even had prayers that there might be no Samaritans in the second resurrection. In other words, because of long standing hostility, they hated Samaritans so much that they prayed that all Samaritans might go to Hell.

Contrary to Jewish popular opinion and nationalistic views, however, Jesus taught that God was not bound to human thinking. His love was not restrained to one people group; instead, it overflowed to the entire world. God loves Jews, and He loves Samaritans. He loves Asians, Africans, Americans, Europeans, the young, the old, the rich, the poor—the world. God looks upon the world He created, and the people He formed from the dust, and He loves the work of His hands. Despite the desolation sin wrought on the world, despite the many evils that humanity had committed, God still looked down from Heaven and declared His deep love for all people.

The Savior vs the Condemner

In close connection with this verse, Jesus follows up His statement with a one-two punch. First, He announces, "For God did not send his Son into the world to condemn the world, but to save the world through him" (John 3:17). Had God wanted to send condemnation, He would have sent Jesus with words akin to those He had given Isaiah. Humanity deserved nothing less. Even so, God did not send Jesus as a condemner; He sent Him as the Savior; born in a manger and hung on a tree.

Second, while Jesus came to save, He told Nicodemus that "Whoever believes in Him is not condemned, but whoever does not believe stands condemned already because they have not believed in the name of God's one and only Son" (John 3:18). Jesus affirms that, at this time, while He has not come to condemn, there would be an appointed time in the future where He would return; and, on that day, hope of salvation would cease. In that hour, those who rejected the salvation He offered will receive the consequences of their choice.

Conclusion

As a Gentile convert, I take comfort in Jesus' words concerning salvation: that someone like me, who is not a descendant of Abraham, might be welcomed into the kingdom of God. Sadly, this pedigree-focused type of thinking has permeated the way many people perceive salvation even today.

Some Christian denominations in particular teach that if one is born into a Christian family, or if one attends church services on a regular basis, then he will be saved. Jesus was loving and honest enough, however, to dispute such narcissistic viewpoints. His rebuke, though, did not come without hope. Jesus extended the regenerative power of the Holy Spirit to every man and woman. Four times in His conversation with Nicodemus, Jesus used the words "whoever" and "everyone" in a positive light to emphasize the inclusivity of salvation.

The kingdom of God is not reserved for Jews only, but rather, Heaven's gates are open to every individual who is reborn. The Way up came down that we might know how to receive this new birth and join with Heaven's throng as people from every nation, tribe, and tongue give praise to the Savior who offers us new life.

XI: FIGS AND THORNS

Date: c. AD 28
Location: Mount Karn Hattin, Capernaum

Soon after His ministry began, Jesus' radical message of hope began to build momentum. In no time at all, He became a household name, a celebrity among the people. Yet, Jesus did not come into the world seeking celebrity status. Rather, Jesus came to bear witness to the truth, the *full* truth. Thus, with this goal in mind, and to combat the false teachings of the Jews concerning their narcissistic self-righteousness, Jesus ascended Mount Karn outside Capernaum.

Capernaum had served as the headquarters for the early months of Jesus' ministry, but the city was too small for the crowds that Jesus drew. For this reason, and others, Jesus hoped that Mount Karn might serve as a suitable place for delivering His next discourse. Ascending the mountain, perhaps Jesus reminisced over how similar His actions mirrored those of the prophet Moses millennia before Him. Just as Moses ascended Mount Sinai to deliver God's law as God's representative, so

Jesus ascended Mount Karn to deliver God's message as God in the flesh.

When He had reached a desirable point near the mountain's summit, Jesus sat down and waited for His disciples to draw near. He then inhaled deeply and surveyed the surrounding masses. Crowds of men, women, and children flocked around Him, completely disregarding their work that they might hear His words. Yearning with compassion for His people, Jesus sighed heavily with concern for them. He knew that many of them held fast to erroneous doctrines stating that salvation and reconciliation with God might be obtained by mere biology, as Nicodemus once believed. Simply because they were children of Abraham, most Jews believed they were entitled to God's grace. But Jesus refused to allow them to labor further under such false delusions. It was time that they knew that salvation was tied neither to human biology nor to good works, but rather it was the product of God's incredibly gracious sacrifice.

The Impossible Standard

The prophetic eloquence epitomized in Jesus' philosophical and theological discourse surpassed that of former great thinkers such as Plato and Confucius. For from the opening of His mouth in verse 2, Jesus delivered the unparalleled wisdom of the Most High. He who was the wisdom of God (1 Cor. 1:24) and the Word of God (John 1:1-3) spoke with authority on a broad range of issues, civil, ceremonial, and religious.

Jesus was not a polished lawyer or politician, who hid His agenda and conformed to the political correctness of the era. He did not carefully craft His message to curry their favor.

Rather, Jesus distanced Himself from the self-righteous and identified the corruption at the root of society.

Jesus' sermon centered on the need for righteousness and the ways in which His disciples might be declared righteous. After acknowledging external sins, Jesus delved deeper. He identified internal sins as equal to external ones; for example, He made no distinction between anger and murder or lust and adultery. In so doing, future scholars postulated that Jesus presented an impossible standard to His listeners. Because Jesus did not shy from the truth, His initial words about observable behaviors were probably met with interest, while His observations about one's thought life likely raised many eyebrows.

Jesus' listeners realized that He was calling for nothing less than perfection. It was challenging enough not to sin with their mouths, but now they must not sin even in their minds. How could this be done? No doubt, many listeners viewed Jesus as no different from the unsympathetic theologians and philosophers before Him, men who preached lofty words but lacked empathy towards their audience. Yet, Jesus proved authoritative on all matters. He did not simply teach like learned men before Him, but rather He preached as one with power. Thus, His listeners were eager to hear what He had to say.

With the crowd hanging on His every word, Jesus spoke at length on many weighty matters. Finally, before He closed His most famous sermon, He addressed one last issue, one final false notion He desired to dispel.

The Scariest Verse in the Bible

Up to this point in His message, Jesus had laid out a number of principles. At first, His words engendered encouragement and interest among His listeners. In verse 21, however, His tone shifted.

"Not everyone who says to me, 'Lord, Lord,' will enter the kingdom of Heaven, but only the one who does the will of my Father who is in Heaven" (Matt. 7:21).

Wait…what? If I were one of Jesus' Jewish listeners, I would have been greatly confused. *You mean to say that even if I call Him "Lord," I still may not be permitted into Heaven?*

Significantly, while the confession of Jesus as Lord with one's mouth is necessary for salvation (Rom. 10:9-10), confession with one's life is equally critical. In other words, a person's actions confirm his beliefs. As James put it, "[F]aith by itself, if it is not accompanied by action, is dead" (James 2:17). How does one truly treat Jesus as Lord and not just pay Him lip service as such? Well, Jesus Himself says that if we love Him, we will obey His commands. Thus, putting our faith in Jesus Christ involves repentance and obedience, not merely words. As Dr. Chris Gnanakan, author and professor at Liberty University, says, "FAITH is summed up in these words: Forsaking All, I Take Him."

Lord

We often hear in prayers, "Dear, Lord," but what does *Lord* even mean? While the word often occurs in Scripture as a reference to the divine name (YHWH), the term *Lord* itself means both master and owner.[1] Thus, when Jesus claimed to be *Lord*, and His disciples called Him *Lord*, they referred to His mastership and ownership over them (John 20:28).

In this sense, all Jesus' followers are slaves to Him, as Paul would later profess (Rom. 1:1). As slaves, our whole mindset should change concerning our relation to Christ. We no longer live to satisfy our own fleshly desires, but rather, our goals and desires are to be tuned to His.

Jesus' mastery over our souls is implicit in the very nature of redemption. In ancient culture, redemption commonly referred to a purchase at the marketplace. Oftentimes, this reference to redemption occurred when a wealthy man entered the marketplace and purchased a slave. In so doing, he redeemed (bought back) that slave for himself. Similarly, Jesus purchased us in the marketplace of sin with His precious blood. Therefore, we are no longer owned by sin; we have a new master—and it is not ourselves—His name is Jesus.

While our relationship to Christ is starkly different than that of ordinary servitude (for He also calls us *children* and *co-heirs*), and we can approach God's throne with confidence (Heb. 4:16), we must remember our place. He is the Master, He is Lord, and we are His servants. If *we* were the masters, we would have no hope of salvation, but if *He* is the Master, if He is Lord, if we submit ourselves under His will, hope remains.

False Prophets

Even after an initial affirmation of Jesus' Lordship, it is imperative that we continue to live in light of this truth. As noted, many will start off strong and call Jesus "Lord," but they will not finish well. Jesus declared in regard to these people, "Many will say to me on that day, 'Lord, Lord, did we not prophesy in your name[?]'" (Matt. 17:22).

Prophecy in the Bible can mean a number of things, but in this particular passage of Scripture, Jesus utilizes the Greek word *propheteuo*. This word implies foretelling events, speaking under inspiration, and exercising the prophetic office. In terms of this passage, Jesus refers to individuals who invoke God's name and authority in their predictions and teachings. These are men and women who insinuate God's authority and direction, and yet they clearly do not have God's intentions in mind. Rather, they have perverted the truth for a lie, taking the Lord's name in vain to justify their message.

Individuals such as these can be found in all types of churches. False prophets do not come as a shock to followers of Jesus, for Jesus Himself prophesied that false prophets lurk about as wolves in sheep's clothing. Jesus' listeners knew all too well of the dangers shepherds dealt with in protecting their flocks, for wolves often would sneak in among the flocks to devour their prey. Like *Aesop's* cunning wolf who disguised himself in a sheep's skin and prowled amongst the sheep, false prophets conceal their true identity and devious purpose. (Even Satan himself was said to masquerade as an angel of light.) Their concern is not for God or His Word but for what they can gain for themselves. Thus, Jesus commands His followers not to reason with these false prophets but to expel them immediately from their midst.

Unfortunately, rather than expelling false prophets, modern-day America has embraced them. Crowds pack out stadiums and respond with rapturous applause to false prophets who tickle their ears with promises of wealth and healing if one just gives enough or believes enough. Like slow-acting poison, the potent harm of false prophets may go undetected at first but give it time. Many of us adamantly claim that we would never drink from a bottle with 99% water and 1% poison. If so, why are we willing to swallow the teachings of false teachers whose deceit is far more detrimental to our soul than cyanide is to our body?

These men and women who invoke the name of God before men in their erroneous teachings will be called to answer before God's throne of judgment. Men who claim to propagate Jesus and yet undermine His nature and purpose shall plead, "Lord, did we not prophesy in your name? Did we not tell the masses about you? Did we not lead many to you?" In wrath, God will look upon them and condemn them in accordance with their offense (1 Cor. 11:15). They sought to popularize the broad road, the one which leads to destruction, and in so doing, they blinded the masses to the truth. For this great evil, they will be judged most harshly. The truth may not always be popular, it may not always be appealing, it may not always draw crowds, but in the end, the knowledge of the truth is the only way by which an individual can enter into the grace of Jesus.

Exorcisms

The text moves to a second group of people who cry out asking if they did not in God's name "drive out demons" (Matt 7:22).

This passage is one of the most frightening in all Scripture. Here Jesus did not condemn blatant unbelievers, murderers, or serious criminals. Rather, He condemned those who appeared at surface level to have put their faith in Him -- those who cast out demons! Why would Jesus condemn such people?

All recorded incidents of exorcism in the New Testament occurred only within the knowledge and will of God. The New Testament records several failed exorcisms (Acts 19) as a way of showing that exorcism is not something to be taken lightly. Demons are powerful spiritual beings who will not flee merely because of one's invocation of Christ's name (Acts 19). Rather, they seem to have the ability to discern God's power exhibited by an individual and will only flee if God truly wills it (Matt. 17:16).

A successful exorcism can be attributed to nothing less than the power of God, and since God's name cannot be taken in vain in the circumstance of exorcism, it is implied that exorcisms can be performed by only true believers. Thus, when Jesus declared that He denied entry into Heaven for individuals who performed exorcisms, it brought alarm to His listeners.

How can those who cast out demons, a seemingly plausible sign of a strong relationship with Christ, face divine judgment and eternal damnation? How can those who cast out demons be condemned to the places to which all demons will be banished?

This is a frightening warning on Jesus' part, for He teaches that while God may be pleased to work through unsaved individuals for His glory, solely because He uses that individual as an instrument does not mean that the individual in question is credited as righteous. That individual must still repent of his or her sin and submit entirely to the Father's will by trusting in Jesus Christ. Otherwise, he will be punished, alongside the demons he exorcised, in the second death.

Performing Miracles

Lastly, Jesus names the third group of people who ask if in Jesus' name they did not "perform many miracles" (Matt. 7:22). Outside His death, burial, and resurrection, Jesus Himself is most famous for His miracles. He was and is a Miracle-worker.

So, those who perform miracles more often than not reflect this aspect of Jesus.

Jesus does not condemn these miracles as done by the power of Satan, but rather, He condemns the intentions of the miracles. Those who performed such miracles did not do so for Jesus' glory, but for their own. To this extent, there are many televangelists who call on individuals to throw aside their crutches and walk in the hopes of boosting the televangelists' funding and raising their viewer count. They look not for the affirmation of God but for the praise of men; thus, they shall receive exactly what it is they hoped to gain. Men will look on them with approval, but the Father will condemn their works as attributed to selfish interest.

Desperation

All these types of people seem to exhibit behaviors of people we would expect to be admitted into Heaven. When was the last time you prophesied? Did you ever exorcise a demon? Perhaps you performed a mighty miracle?

Notice the desperation of these people. They cry out to Jesus, "Lord, Lord, did we not…" They are adamant. Their condemnation blindsides them. This was not the first time they referred to Jesus as "Lord." They did not simply call Him "Lord" in hopes of escaping judgment, rather they emphatically confessed Jesus as "Lord" before men. They danced and called Him "Lord," they sang and called Him "Lord," they prayed and called Him "Lord," and yet He knew them not. Their profession was not a genuine confession of their heart!

A Solemn Warning

Sadly, today, many people want to be spiritual but not religious. The modern-day church blasts religion as a man-centered, ritualistic construct and says, "Christianity is a relationship, not a religion." What many mean by saying this is that "I don't need to follow a set of rules, I can just have a relationship with Jesus." That position assumes, however, that there are no rules, no manners of protocol, in that relationship. Jesus makes it very clear that those who love Him will keep His commands (John 14:15). You cannot have a relationship with Him and act like the world. Man-made religion is evil, but God-ordained religion is holy.

So many people, especially young people, want to experience the power of God without truly adhering to the word of God. They believe in private interpretation, private revelation, private this, and private that, but what God has made public to all people, they shun. Instead, they profess that what God has made private to them supersedes that which He has made public to everyone else. In other words, they become like the Israelites whom Paul addresses in his letter to the church in Rome: "They have a zeal for God, but not in accordance with knowledge" (Rom. 10:2).

To obey God is greater than sacrifice (1 Sam. 15:22). God esteems submissive obedience to His commands as more pleasing in His sight than exorcisms and miracles done apart from Him. God does not desire a "spiritual" people. He desires a holy one.

Already, I hear the objections. Some charismatic teachers claim that lives are changed only through signs and wonders. Jesus disagreed, not only in this sermon but countless other times when He Himself performed miracles.

When Jesus fed the five thousand, they loved the miracle! Yet, when Jesus tied the miracle to a message, they left Him (John 6:66). They lacked the desire to practice what He preached. They came not for a life change but a life experience! Further proof of this exists when Jesus healed ten lepers, yet only one returned to Him to thank Him. If signs and wonders are what change lives, then all ten lepers should have returned to Jesus and emphatically praised Him. That is not what happened (Luke 17:17).

This same danger exists today, and many young people, many of my friends, are taking the bait. They want to speak in the tongues of angels, they want to heal on command, but what they do not want to do is obey God's commands. "That's legalistic," they say. Their mindset essentially is, "Forget about the words God says in His book, let's talk about the words I say when I pray!" Is this really what God wants?

Mighty Works vs Mighty Faith

One would think that it is the Father's will for Jesus' followers to prophesy, cast out demons, and perform miracles, but what the Father wants more than anything is for genuine followers to trust in His Son. It does not matter how much you do or how much you say unless your heart is right with God (1 Cor. 13:1-13; Prov. 21:2). Our relationship with God is based on what Jesus has done for us, not on what we have done for Jesus. We can do nothing on our own to earn a relationship with Him (John 15:4), for people are not saved by their works but by the grace of God alone (Eph. 2:8-9).

In this passage, Jesus refuted the idea of working one's way to Heaven or attempting to please God through mighty feats.

God is more pleased by those who do no such works yet have genuine love for Him than by those who perform mighty miracles and lack such love.

I Never Knew You

Being both omniscient and omnipresent, God knows all and sees all. Thus, He does not deny that He is aware of the deeds of such individuals, but He unequivocally declares that He never truly had a relationship with them. Many people exist of whom I have heard and have never met, and while I can say that I know *about* such individuals, I cannot say that I actually *know* them. So, it shall be for those who do not have a genuine relationship with Christ. That is how distant He shall be from them.

He will proclaim, "I never knew you. I never gave you My stamp of approval. There was no communication between us. You speak of these great things you have done for me, yet, as they were done for your own glory, I played no part in your works. In name only was I a part of your life. I was never genuinely a part of your life, so why should you expect that I should make you a part of Mine?"

This is why the most important thing in life is not that *you* know Jesus. It's not. Many people today profess to know Jesus, and they preach from the pulpit, serve on the mission field, and attend Bible studies. While they may be associated with Christ, for some of them, their hearts are far from Him. He will say unto them, "Depart from me, ye that work iniquity" (Matt. 7:23, KJV).

The most important thing in life is that *Jesus* knows you. I may know the president of the United States, but just because

I know him does not mean that the secret service will admit me into the White House. But, if the president knows me, I do not have to try to get in. I am already invited. In the same way, you will be permitted into Heaven only if Jesus knows you!

The Absence of God's Presence

This is the greatest punishment an individual can ever receive: to be banished from the presence of God. Human beings are made to desire to be with God. While on Earth, they receive the benefits of God's presence, even if they foolishly seek to replace it with lesser substitutes. Thus, the worst thing a person can experience is the withdrawal of God's presence. The most severe punishment of Hell is not fire and torment but the complete separation of an individual from God's benevolence. Only then, after a man is judged, will he come to the realization that what he was missing in his life the whole time was recognizing the presence of God. How sad that it will be too late for that person to beg for forgiveness.

Workers of Iniquity

Such people who profess Jesus but whom He does not know are labeled as "workers of iniquity." Iniquity refers not to an action but to a condition of character. Murderers, thieves, and adulterers are most commonly known to be workers of iniquity. But here, Jesus said that those who preached, exorcised, and performed miracles in His name, yet did so for their own glory, they shall receive justice in full. In fact, they worked more iniquity than the murderers and adulterers, for they exchanged the truth for a lie and poisoned the minds of others into believing a false gospel.

Tellingly, when questioned before the throne of God, they did not beg for mercy or forgiveness. Instead, they attempted to justify their actions. "Did we not do this, and did we not do that?" Even till the end their focus was on themselves rather than on Christ. In response, Jesus said (to paraphrase), "It doesn't matter what you did. Nothing you do, even if you were to prophesy, cast out demons, or perform miracles, is good enough to get you into Heaven. It's not about what you can do. It's about what I have done for you!"

Unlike a parable, this account is actually a sneak peek Jesus provides into future events. The sad reality is that many people today can replace those same people in the story with themselves, for even some reading this book know that they have a form of godliness, but they lack the real thing. Jesus is not deceived. He knows what is genuine and what is artificial. You can fool others, you can even fool yourself, but you cannot fool God. On the last day, He will judge true faith from a facade (2 Tim. 3:5).

Jesus is the great separator. He separated the seas of the earth from the sky, He separated the Jews from the Egyptians, He separated humanity from the penalty of sin, and He shall separate the faithful from the faithless (Matt. 13:36-43, 47-50; 25:32-33). How sad it would be for Him to separate you from Himself.

Fruits and Roots

So how can you be sure that Jesus will welcome you into Heaven? How do you know that Jesus knows you? Jesus said that you will know them by their fruits (Matt. 7:16). We say today that you cannot judge a book by its cover, but Jesus did not say that. In fact, He said the opposite. You can judge a book by its cover.

Immediately, there are those of us who object. "Who are you to judge? You don't know my heart. In fact, I may not look or act like a Christian, but in my heart, I love and trust in Jesus."

Jesus begged to differ. The Bible teaches that we will be judged by our words (Matt. 12:37), for our words reveal the desires of our hearts (Luke 6:45). While modern culture sees the heart as the center of emotions, the Bible places the heart at the seat of the will. For us to say that we love Jesus in our heart, and yet there is no life change is for us to claim that Jesus has changed our will, but that change has not affected how we will live. Either we are insane or lying!

To illustrate this point, imagine the following scenario. You are supposed to meet your friend at your local favorite restaurant. You arrive on time and patiently wait for your friend to show up. Minutes pass and he still does not arrive. You text, no answer. Finally, a half an hour late, your friend walks up to your table.

"Where were you?" you ask. "Why didn't you answer my text?"

"Oh, I am so sorry!" your friend replies. "I was on my way here and I saw a turtle crossing the road. I stopped my car, got out, scooped up the turtle and brought him into the nearby woods. On my way back to my car, a tractor trailer came barreling down the road at what had to be 100 miles per hour and ran right over me!"

You look him over, notice his unblemished appearance, and declare, "Have you gone crazy? Why are you lying?"

Your friend protests incredulously, "Why don't you believe me?"

You inspect him carefully. No blood, not even a scratch. "You're a liar, man!" you reply.

"Why? What's so hard to believe?" he asks.

"There is no way in the world you could have had such an encounter with a tractor trailer and still look the same!"

Then why do we believe is it possible for us to have an encounter with God and remain unchanged? Is a tractor trailer more powerful than God?

Knowing God changes us. And that change from the inside produces a change on the outside. As Jesus explained, people are known by their fruit. Jesus asks His listeners in Matthew 7, "Do people pick grapes from thornbushes?" (Matt. 7:16).

I can picture His listeners answering in their head, "Of course not, Jesus. You won't find grapes on thornbushes. Grapes grow on grape trees. You'll only find thorns on thornbushes."

Next, Jesus asks, "Or figs from thistles?" (Matt. 7:16).

"Right again, Jesus," the onlookers must have thought. "Anyone who thinks they can find figs on thistles is either lying or insane!"

Then, Jesus drops the mic: "Likewise, every good tree bears good fruit, but a bad tree bears bad fruit. A good tree cannot bear bad fruit, and a bad tree cannot bear good fruit" (Matt. 7:17-18). In other words, anyone who comes to Jesus claiming to be a Christian, and yet, whose actions are inconsistent with that profession, Jesus says that they are either lying or insane! You will be known by your fruit. So, what fruit are you bearing?

Time's Up!

A time will come when it will be too late for an individual to come to the saving knowledge of faith in Jesus Christ. No human being has unlimited time at his or her disposal. No one knows the day nor the hour when God will say, "Time's up!" It could be ten years from now or it could be today. Only God knows.

The urgency of the Gospel relies on this bedrock truth, that judgment is coming, and it can arrive at any time. The wise man prepares for this inevitable appointment.

In the case of the people Jesus condemned as workers of iniquity, they had readied themselves poorly for such a day. They placed the emphasis of their faith on their outward works rather than the inner work of the heart. In so doing, they denied the Holy Spirit the ability to reside in their hearts, and so, they condemned themselves.

So as not to fall into the same trap, believers in Jesus should not only do the good works Jesus called us to do, but it is equally important that we reflect on our intimate, personal relationship with Jesus. Ask ourselves probing questions and give ourselves honest answers. Do I truly trust God? Am I drawing nearer to Him? Do I have an artificial faith, or a faith built on a solid foundation? Would He say He knows me? Pray that the Holy Spirit exposes any self-deceit, for while we can fool ourselves, we certainly cannot fool God.

In the end, we each will be held accountable for our own lives. We cannot stop others from living the way they choose, but we can make our own choices. It is imperative, therefore, that we remember this truth, for what a shame it would be if we would lead others to Jesus, and yet He would not have root in our own hearts.

Conclusion

The way of salvation Jesus sets forth in the Gospels and extrapolates on in His Sermon on the Mount stands in stark contrast to that which we witness today. Today, we try to categorize what it means to follow Jesus in a checklist. Do you want to go to Heaven? Yes. Do you know you are a sinner? Yes. Do you want to ask Jesus to come into your heart? Yes. Did you ask Him into your heart? Yes. Then you are saved! There is no true life change; instead, there is a dependence on the sincerity of one's decision. No longer do we trust in Jesus, instead, we trust in a moment! This unsubstantiated method of evangelism cannot be found in Scripture or church history at all!

Today, easy 'believism' has become the norm in many churches, whereby someone is saved merely by accepting a set number of facts. Jesus never taught that. Jesus told us to deny ourselves, take up our cross, and follow Him (Matt. 16:24).

Jesus was not interested in fans—He sought disciples. What's the difference? A fan will go to church on Sunday, buy Christian T-shirts, download Christian songs, and listen to Christian sermons. A follower is willing to forsake everything for Jesus. Fans come and go; when their team is not winning, they switch over. A disciple, though, is loyal till the end.

Jesus said, "You want to know what a true follower of mine looks like? Deny yourself, take up your cross, and follow me!" That is true discipleship, and that is what Jesus is after. God wants our devotion, not our commotion. Fans bear banners; disciples carry crosses. Prophesies, exorcisms, and miracles are all empty if He is not at the center. Thus, true faith is summed up with what we do with Jesus, for what we do with Jesus will ultimately determine what He does with us. C. S. Lewis said this: "There are only two kinds of people in the end: those who say to God, 'Thy will be done,' and those to whom God says, in the end, 'Thy will be done.'" Which will you be?

XII: IN MONEY WE TRUST

Date: c. AD 28
Location: Perea, east of the Jordan River

Jesus' disciples closed in around Him as Jesus and His followers started along the long road towards Jerusalem. Unbeknownst to them, every step Jesus took was one step closer to the cross. He was born for this purpose, that He should one day be crucified outside of Jerusalem. Jesus did not resist His Father's plan but entrusted Himself to His Father's care.

Joy overwhelmed Jesus' soul when, only moments prior, children crowded around Him, longing simply to be in His presence. If only all Jesus' followers were like these children, understanding the joy that came with being in close proximity to Jesus. In fact, it was for this purpose that Jesus set out to Jerusalem, to reconcile all humanity to Himself that they might indeed become the children of God. Thus, the Everlasting Father trekked onward for the love He had for His children. No human being deserved this inexpressible love, but Jesus chose to extend it anyway -- to both children and adults alike.

Sure enough, as Jesus was walking on His way, speaking with His disciples, He heard a voice cry out to Him from the midst of the crowd. "Good Teacher!"

Jesus ground to a halt, along with all His traveling companions. His eyes roamed the sea of people, searching for a sign of the speaker. Shortly thereafter, a young man suddenly raced through the crowd, adorned in wealth and followed by servants. This man had heard about Jesus of Nazareth. He was said to be unlike the other rabbis of His day or even those before Him.

Attracted to Jesus' radical dogma, the man ignored those in his inner circle who dismissed Jesus as a ranting pauper lacking proper pedigree. As a rich ruler, this man had access to a vast array of resources answering all of life's questions, a luxury the poor did not possess. Yet, despite his vast library, the ruler purposed to venture from his scrolls in search of Him who was the Word.

Unsatisfied with what Plato, Aristotle, or the other philosophers and rabbis postulated, he actively sought the wisdom of Jesus. So sure was he that Jesus held the answer to his question, he refused to send a servant in his stead. Determined, he left his palace so that he might learn the truth.

Upon finally coming face to face with Jesus, the rich young ruler did not seek to impress the Nazarene rabbi. In the sight of his servants and Jesus' disciples alike, he immediately knelt before Jesus, acknowledging Jesus' superiority.

Meeting Jesus

Very few Jews during Jesus' earthly ministry dignified Jesus by kneeling before Him. This partly stemmed from Jewish history where Jews were famous for their reverence shown only to God. Jews like Mordecai went so far as to face the prospect of death for refusing to bow to royal officials (Esther 3:4). Yet, the rich young ruler, one whom culture deemed others should have bowed to, prostrated himself before Jesus.

Jesus did not have servants like the ruler, nor armed guards, but the rich young ruler recognized something in Jesus akin to himself. Jesus, like He, was a ruler, but unlike the rich young ruler, Jesus possessed something that could not be bought by money. Seeking this treasure, the man prostrated himself and asked Jesus, "Good Teacher, what must I do to inherit eternal life?" (Mark 10:17).

Seeking Jesus

This mysterious, unnamed individual who approached Jesus is known in the Bible only as a "rich young ruler." By worldly accounts, he seemed to have it all, not just health and not just wealth, but both. But he did not seem to adhere to the pseudo-Prosperity Gospel common in his day. During Biblical times, Jews believed that you reaped what you sowed. If you were blessed by God, then it was a sign of your righteousness; but if you were lame, crippled, or poor, it was a sign of your sin. Based on his actions, the ruler seemed to doubt this way of thinking. Despite having both, something inside him told him that there was more to life than youth and money. So, he made a wise decision—he sought out the source of truth.

Upon meeting Jesus, the man asked, "Good Teacher, what must I do to inherit eternal life?" (Mark 10:17). While Jesus had often been referred to as "teacher," the rich young ruler attached the word "good." In so doing, he was not saying that

Jesus was a skilled teacher, but that Jesus was a teacher who was also good (righteous). Most Jews would have looked at the fortunate circumstances of the ruler's life and accredited him as more righteous than Jesus.

Yet, the man realized that Jesus was unlike himself or the rabbis of his day. Jesus was *good*. Something inside the man clicked to where he registered the purity in Jesus. The Pharisees mocked Him and accused Him of demonic possession, but the rich young ruler christened Him as holy and upright, as good.

Eternity Focused

Significantly, the rich young ruler asked Jesus the only question that really matters. He was not like the Pharisees who asked Jesus trivial questions or riddles intended to trap Him, but rather, he asked the most important question of all: how does one receive eternal life?

Eternal life is exactly that, everlasting existence. Such a concept is boggling to the human mind. If we truly set aside our religious convictions and simply mull over the suggestion of a life without end, I would be the first to confess that the notion of life without end is difficult to conceive. I have seen the leaves wither, the grass die, human beings pass from the earth, and yet Jesus taught that those who put their faith in Him will have life everlasting full of bliss and harmony. If this is true, which of course it is, this is the greatest joy of all.

The Jews of Jesus' day were split with some (the Sadducees) denying the concept of life after death while others (the Pharisees) affirming such a reality. Rather than scoff at the idea of eternal life, like so many of his wealthy peers, the rich man pursued the answer to his most heartfelt question. Despite his riches, despite his fame, and despite his power, he realized that he wanted eternal life. It was not out of a greedy spirit that he came before Jesus, but out of a genuine one. In contrast to most of us, he had a pressing focus on eternity. This motivated him to seek understanding that he could not find at home. Thus, he left his comfort zone in search of Jesus for answers.

Never Good Enough

As mentioned, upon meeting Jesus, who does not deny the rich young ruler an audience, the man calls Jesus "Good Teacher." Immediately, Jesus counters the man's claim: "Why do you call Me good? No one is good – except God alone" (Mark 10:18). On the surface, Jesus' response seems to be somewhat confrontational. Jesus is indeed good, beyond any doubt, so why did He respond as He did? If we examine Jesus' statements carefully, we will find that He is attempting to enable the man to see a greater truth.

We have no indication that the rich young ruler believes Jesus to be God in the flesh. Thus, Jesus tries to lead the man to see the full picture. God is the standard of goodness. Period. Jesus, of course, is God, but since the man does not know that, Jesus tries to show the man the impossibility of humanity attaining that standard without God's help.

The sad truth is that many of us believe that we are good enough on our own. Benjamin Franklin, a professed atheist, claimed that while he does not believe in the existence of God, he does believe that if there were a God, that God would allow him into Heaven based on his contribution to society. In other words, Benjamin Franklin placed the weight of his hope on his good works.

Many of us are like Benjamin Franklin. We tend to minimize our sins and maximize our "good" works. The majority of world religions hold this view, that if an individual's good works outweigh his misdeeds, he will enter some form of paradise. The Bible says otherwise.

The Book of Romans clearly states that "all have sinned and fall short of the glory of God" (Rom. 3:23). This idea of falling short, of missing the mark, is known in the Hebrew language as *khata*. *Khata* is to miss God's perfect mark. The Bible teaches that we have all missed that mark of absolute perfection. Additionally, according to Romans 6:23, "For the wages of sin is death[.]" Each and every single human being, no matter how seemingly kind and generous, is guilty and deserving of death. None of us are capable of reaching that perfect standard, and so, Jesus attempts to destroy the rich young ruler's presupposition from the beginning in hopes that he might not lean on it like a crutch.

The purpose of Jesus and His teachings can be summed up in the realization that only God could fully keep all the rules. No human being could live the perfect life required by the law due to the inherited sin nature of Adam (Rom. 5:12). So, Jesus accomplished for us what we could not do ourselves. Our good works are as filthy rags, but He offers to exchange our works with His. The exchange rate of our works to His is astronomical. We would be fools not to accept such a gracious offer!

Even so, on the Last Day when God questions each and every human being as to why He should allow them into Heaven, many will answer, "I did…" or "I was…" or "I gave…"

The use of first-person pronouns to justify oneself on the day of judgment is futile. Any answer having to do with one's abilities or works is bound to end in damnation, but he who acknowledges that Jesus is the answer, He will be saved.

It is no coincidence that several verses earlier, Jesus said to His disciples, "Truly I tell you, anyone who will not receive the kingdom of God like a little child will never enter it" (Mark 10:15).

As children, penniless, insignificant, and powerless, we must stand before the Almighty and acknowledge our dependence, our sheer inability to do anything good by ourselves. We must confess with our mouths that we are unworthy, but that He in us is so worthy! Only then will God look upon us with a smile and bless us. For those who submit themselves under His mercy and grace are truly children of the kingdom.

Works-Based Faith

The vast majority of world religions today teach that to receive a ticket into Paradise, an individual must pay his own fare. There is, however, an inherent contradiction in this belief system.

If entrance into Heaven requires good works, and if people do such works to get to Heaven, can those works be considered truly good? In other words, can good works come from selfish motives? In this paradigm, people actually operate out of self-interest by doing something for another to gain Heaven for themselves.

J.D. Greear, Pastor of Summit Church, illustrates the dilemma in works-based salvation by relating the following story set in medieval times. As was custom, a certain, beloved king sat on his throne and admitted his subjects one-by-one to hear their pleas. One man, a poor carrot farmer, bowed before the king and said, "Your majesty, I'm a poor carrot farmer. I have very little, but I dug up a four-and-a-half-foot carrot, and when I saw that carrot I thought, 'That's a carrot only fit for a king.' I love you, and I am devoted to you, and you are an awesome king, and I want to give it to you as an emblem of my devotion."

Being genuinely moved by the farmer's gesture, the king asked, "Where do you live?"

The carrot farmer told him, and the king said, "It just so happens that I own all the farmland around your little farm, and because you are such a good subject, and because you bring such delight to my heart, I'm going to give you all that farmland."

And he quadrupled the size of the man's little farm.

And one of the noblemen, standing near the back of the court, heard this and thought, *Wow, if that's what the king would give in response to a carrot, imagine what he would give in response to a real gift like a horse.*

So he went out and found the most magnificent horse in the kingdom and brought the horse in the next day and said, "O king, you're an awesome king, and I love serving you, and you're so wise, and I thought you should have this magnificent horse as an emblem of my devotion to you."

The shrewd, wise king said, "Well, yesterday, the carrot farmer was giving a carrot to me. Today, you're giving a horse to yourself."

This is one of the chief problems for works-based religions, for these religions must justify their dilemma of self-serving "sacrifice." If an individual serves God to earn

Heaven, then does he actually love God or others? Or instead does he love himself?

For the sake of argument, let us overlook this dilemma and assume that someone could actually perform a selfless "good" work apart from God, though we know he cannot (Heb. 11:6). Let us further assume that our good works are not filthy rags in his sight, though we know they are (Is. 46:4). The question becomes, if God is holy, just, and perfect (which He is) how many good works are enough to outweigh our bad works?

To illustrate this concept, imagine that you own a shop, and one night a man breaks into your store and steals some of your valuable merchandise. You bring the man to court, hoping to secure repayment. The thief pleads not guilty. Instead, he says, "Your honor, I know I took the stuff, but you should see all the good I do. I'm a good husband. I'm a good father. I pay my taxes. I don't speed…"

You probably would not care about the man's list of good deeds, would you? You would be focused on exacting justice. And if the judge pardoned the man, you would deem the judge unjust.

In the same way, every sin demands a consequence. God would be unjust if He simply pardoned us in the courtroom of Heaven because of some good deeds we did. No matter how many good deeds we perform, we ultimately fall short of God's perfect standard (Rom. 3:23).

The Law

Noteworthy, however, when Jesus tells the rich man how to receive eternal life, He does not tell Him to live by faith. Rather, He says, "You know the commandments: 'Do not murder, do not commit adultery, do not steal, do not give false testimony, do not defraud, honor your father and mother'" (Mark 10:19).

Why is Jesus bringing up the law if we are saved by grace? Why does Jesus draw a connection between commandments and eternal life? I thought the purpose of the law was to show us our sin not to give us life?

Jesus answers in this way because He is still drawing the man into the heart of the matter. He is answering the man honestly. The man did not ask Jesus, "What must be done to receive eternal life?" Instead, he asked, "What must *I* do?"

To accomplish salvation on his own, the man must keep the law to the letter. There is no other way on his own by which he can receive eternal life.

Jesus is a man of honesty. He will meet us where we are, and so here, He attempts to show the rich young ruler the desperation of his current circumstances. Yes, he can receive eternal life, but only if he keeps the law perfectly.

Rather than despairing, the rich young ruler seems to rejoice. Counting the commandments on his fingers, he searches the depths of his mind for any vague recollections of misdeeds. He then answers Jesus, "Teacher, all these things I have kept since I was a boy" (Mark 10:20).

In this moment, the rich young ruler shows his lack of understanding of when Jesus first rebuked Him. Jesus told the man that only God is good, and now, the rich young ruler is effectively saying, "I am, too!"

Giving him the benefit of the doubt, perhaps the man honestly believed he did not commit any of these particular sins or he did not recall having done so. Obviously, being a human being, the rich young ruler was not without sin. But let us assume he genuinely believed that he had actually kept these commandments. *Hallelujah!* he must have thought to himself. *I did it! I will receive eternal life!*

Love that Gives Attention

The text says, "Jesus looked at him and loved him" (Mark 10:21).

He did not yell, "Liar!" and recount to the crowd the man's many sins. Rather, upon looking at the ruler, He saw another of His beloved so close to coming home. Here he was, in the presence of his Maker, and out of His love for the man, Jesus imparted to him the full truth.

Jesus could have cut His conversation short. He could have dismissed the man and continued on His way. Instead, He took time to listen to the rich young ruler, showing the love He had for him. When Jesus looked at the man, He did not see his riches, He did not see his prestige; He saw one of His Creation, formed in His own image. Looking upon this man, Jesus lovingly sought to set him free from his misconceptions.

The Honest Teacher

Had Jesus sent the rich young ruler away with this false hope of righteousness, the man might have gone home and died with no hope of salvation. Upon being judged guilty before God's throne, he would have been utterly confused. He would have understandably argued, "But Jesus said all I needed to do was obey the laws! I did obey them! He lied to me."

Jesus is not a conman. He does not try to deceive us or give us false hope. Instead, He presents the truth personally, in a way His listeners can grasp if they are willing to listen.

Addressing the rich young ruler, Jesus said, "One thing you lack...Go, sell everything you have and give to the poor, and you will have treasure in heaven. Then come, follow Me" (Mark 10:21).

Jesus does not challenge the man's answer. He does not accuse Him of lying or deceiving himself. Instead, He presents the rich young ruler with a test of faith: which is worth more to you, money or eternal life?

Jesus was not asking for a donation to the Jesus Foundation, whereby the ruler might be entitled to a memorial erected in his honor. Rather, Jesus commanded the man to give to the poor, people unable to reciprocate monetarily. In exchange, Jesus curiously did not promise the man eternal life. No one can buy salvation – it is a gift. But should the ruler give up his wealth, he might allow himself to be open to receiving this gift. What Jesus did promise was treasures in Heaven, an exchange beyond all exchanges.

Jesus was accustomed to the exorbitant exchange rates whereby money changers would essentially rob Jews offering sacrifices at the Temple. Jesus, however, was offering the ruler the ultimate prize! This was his chance to win big. It was almost as if Jesus was holding something behind His back, ready and willing to hand it over, should the man accept the terms.

Unable to see the treasure laid up for him in Heaven, the ruler refused to take the gamble. It was too high of a risk. Why should he give up all that he had, all that he had worked so hard for, simply to live a life of servitude? The exchange of his temporal treasures for eternal ones seemed to come at too great a cost.

The Bible says that the rich young ruler's "face fell. He went away sad, because he had great wealth" (Mark 10:22).

While Jesus was full of love, the rich young ruler was full of grief. He wanted eternal life, but he did not want it enough. Instead of asking further questions, instead of seeking a way out, he turned and left.

Many people will choose to debate Jesus for hours and even years, attempting to justify their actions, but the rich young ruler was convicted of the truth. He believed Jesus' every word. He did not come hoping to debate, but to learn. He knew that whatever Jesus said was true. But when he learned what the truth was, following it seemed too great a sacrifice.

The Hypocritical Levite

While the Bible does not outrightly identify the rich young ruler's background, a careful exegesis of the Scripture suggests this man may have been a Levite. Jesus was nearing Jericho (a Levitical city), Jesus quoted the second portion of the Decalogue (the first portion would have been fulfilled by virtue of a Levite's calling), and Jesus commanded this man to sell his possessions to the poor. Jesus' command takes on added meaning when viewed in light of this man's background.

Levites "have no share or inheritance among their fellow Israelites; the LORD is their inheritance, as the LORD your God told them" (Lev. 10:9). This means that Levites were not to amass wealth for themselves. If this man were a Levite, he would be a living contradiction of God's command. Thus, when Jesus instructed the man to sell his possessions, this was a call for repentance. Jesus was asking the man to fulfill the oath he had thus far failed to keep, but the man refused.

Conclusion

Contrary to popular belief, Jesus did not shy from the hard topics, addressing money twice as much as He did Heaven. Living below His means, Jesus encouraged His followers, present and future, to seek treasures in Heaven that will never fade. Unfortunately, the enemy encourages the acquisition of material gains in the present age, in the hopes of getting us to forfeit the greater blessing God has in store or us.

Some Prosperity Gospel preachers lead their congregants astray claiming that we can somehow "cash out" our treasures in Heaven, and in a sense, they're right. The more and more we invest in this world, the less and less we invest in the world to come.

Money is not to hinder us. Those who love Jesus cannot also love money. Some ask, "Well, how much is too much?" You tell me. To what do you devote your time, resources, and money? To yourself, or are you giving to the widows and orphans? When your money becomes an asset for your best life now, that should give you pause. Jesus Himself said it plainly, "No one can serve two masters. Either you will hate the one and love the other, or you will be devoted to the one and despise the other. You cannot serve both God and money" (Matt. 6:24). Decide for yourself whether the wealth you procure here should hinder you from the wealth found only in Christ. You can walk away grieved and disheartened like the rich young ruler, or you can forsake all worldly gain and cling to Christ. You cannot buy salvation, nor can you bring your earthly treasures with you into the next life. You must be willing to live for Christ regardless of your circumstances. This is the way! It may be a way of poverty to some, but better to be poor in this world and rich in the next, then to be rich in this world and poor in the next. Which will you choose?

XIII: THIS IS THE WAY

Date: c. AD 30
Location: Upper Room, Jerusalem

Tension builds in the upper room of one of the houses in the Lower City of Jerusalem. Jesus and His disciples lounge around an eighteen-inch high wooden table as they partake in the annual Passover meal. This was the third Passover meal Jesus and His disciples ate together in Jerusalem, but each of them sensed that something was different this evening. Just less than a week ago, when Jesus had entered Jerusalem, He had been welcomed with rapturous applause and honor befitting a king.

His arrival in Jerusalem was something Jesus had foreseen years in advance, but His apostles did not grasp His actual intentions. After three years of ministry, Jesus knew that His time on the earth was drawing to a close. Keenly aware of what lay before Him that same evening, Jesus soberly partook in His final meal with His disciples. At length, Jesus broke His silence, determined that before He left His disciples, He rein-forced the truth of His identity and purpose.

Coexist

The symbol "coexist" has become synonymous with the concept that all religions cannot only live at peace with one another, but that all religions are essentially the same. Inherent in this view is that while all religions may appear superficially different on the *outside*, they are virtually identical on the *inside*. In other words, Christianity, Islam, Bahai, Judaism, Scientology, and the like are all different paths up the same mountain with paradise at the mountain's peak.[16] According to the coexist view, what is important is that all people of different religions learn how to get along with one another in this life.

Such beliefs stand in direct contradiction to Jesus and His teachings. Jesus did not teach a pluralistic, all-roads-lead-to-Heaven doctrine. While Jesus was very clear that His invitation of salvation was all-inclusive (*i.e.*, for everyone), He unmistakably proclaimed that the way to Heaven was indeed limited (*i.e.*, through Him). An examination of Jesus' last discourse with His disciples before His crucifixion highlights His exclusive monopoly on eternal life as the only way to Heaven.

Equality with God

In John 14, while addressing His disciples during their last meal prior to Jesus' crucifixion, Jesus declared, "Do not let your hearts be troubled. You believe in God, believe also in Me" (John 14:1).

What a claim! Had the disciples been truly convinced that Jesus was committing blasphemy, they would have picked up stones and killed Him on the spot, but such was the assurance in their hearts that they knew there was more to this Jewish rabbi than met the eye. Yes, He was their teacher, but He was so much more. He performed miracles unlike anyone else, miracles greater than Elisha and Moses. He taught as one with authority, not as any of the other Jewish leaders. He had never—not once—sinned, and they would have known, having lived with Him for three years. Who was this man? Was He just a man?

The context of Jesus' statement was during the Last Supper, right after Jesus revealed that Peter would deny Him, and another disciple would betray Him. At this revelation, the other disciples began to despair. But Jesus encouraged them not to be troubled. Why? Because He, Jesus, was the bedrock of their faith.

The disciples were called not only to believe in God, and in God's every word, but now, Jesus called them to believe also His every word. Jesus was, in effect, placing Himself on the same level as God. It was insufficient that His disciples had faith in a God they could not see. Now they must have faith in the One whom they could see.

The Father's House

After giving the command to believe in Him, Jesus provides a promise: "My Father's house has many rooms; if that were not so, would I have told you that I am going there to prepare a place for you?" (John 14:2).

In ancient Jewish custom, in preparation for a marriage, the father of the groom incorporated a house extension to accommodate the newlyweds. Likewise, Jesus proclaimed that, in accordance with His impending marriage (Rev. 19:7-9), He would prepare rooms in Heaven for His bride, the church.

Regardless of our age, many of us can recall when we were young and living in our father's house. Those of us who had a loving, hard-working father can remember receiving the blessings of his security and provision. At the time, we lacked responsibility and instead gladly accepted our role as the lesser in the household because we knew our father would take care of us. Likewise, those who enter Heaven will find a loving Father who provides all they need. This is assuring news for many adults who muse over being able to return to the carefree days of youth where they lacked worldly concerns. It is also abundantly comforting when contemplating our own departure from this earth, for death is merely the doorway to the Father's House. Jesus, who speaks of things He Himself has seen, promises us a room in Heaven. There the children of the Most High will enjoy the eternal peace, providence, and provision He has promised those who love Him. And there we will enjoy the biggest treasure of all—God's very own continual presence!

Additionally, what a joy it is to know that there are *many* rooms in Heaven. Indeed, it would be tragic had Jesus said, "In My Father's house are only a couple rooms." This would imply that the way of salvation is reserved for only a select few. But, in stating that there are many rooms, Jesus declares that Heaven is open to the masses. God has not set a maximum capacity, as some, like Jehovah's Witnesses, suggest, but instead, God offers refuge to all those who trust in Him and His Son. All such people are welcome in the Father's House.

The Promised Resurrection of Christ

Jesus had prophesied to His disciples several times concerning His imminent execution, and this night was no different. Here, once again, Jesus reminds His disciples that, while He will be separated from them temporarily, He will return to them once more. When He does, however, He will be clothed in glory akin to that which He possessed before the foundation of the world.

In this manner, Jesus attempts to prepare His disciples for His inevitable departure, and, in the same breath, provide them hope. His leaving is for their eternal benefit. He explains, "And if I go and prepare a place for you, I will come back and take you to be with me that you also may be where I am" (John 14:3). Jesus' death and resurrection are His necessary preparations to ready Heaven for His disciples (and us). They are the required conditions, the keys, if you will, to allowing an individual access into His Father's House. Thus, Jesus commands His disciples to take heart, for His death and resurrection would pave the way for them to be together for eternity.

The Way

When Jesus finishes saying that He is going to prepare a place for them in His Father's house and that He will come back for them, He concludes by stating, "You know the way to the place where I am going" (John 14:4).

Thomas speaks up. "Lord, we don't know where You are going, so how can we know the way?" (John 14:5). Thomas is a realist. Most times when he is mentioned in Scripture, he is willing to speak his mind. He wants to know the truth. We, like Thomas, should ask these pertinent questions when we do not understand, for God is not afraid of being caught off-guard when we press further to learn the truth. He explicitly tells us that if we lack wisdom, we should ask God, and He will give it to us (James 1:5).

Addressing Thomas, Jesus says, "I am the way and the truth and the life. No one comes to the Father except through Me" (John 14:6).

This exclusive statement of Jesus has caused many to label Christianity an intolerant faith, but such could not be further from the truth. To understand what Jesus meant when He claimed to be the way, it is important to first understand what He did *not* mean.

Universalism

Men of the past, such as John Adams, and celebrities of the present, such as Oprah Winfrey, have commonly clung to the viewpoint of universalism, the belief that all humanity will eventually be saved. Universalism exists in the inclusive, syncretic world religions such as Hinduism, Unitarian Universalism, and Bahai, all of which state that all religions eventually lead to the same place.

The common analogy given in support of universalism is the Buddhist parable of the three blind men and an elephant. According to the parable, several blind men come across an elephant and argue over what they have found. One man, feeling the elephant's trunk, thinks it is a snake; another feeling the ear, thinks it is a fan; another feels the leg and thinks it is a tree, and so on down the line.

Universalists love this story because the blind men learn to conceptualize the elephant based on their point of reference.

While each blind man touches a different part of the elephant, they are still touching the same elephant. Their interactions with the elephant may differ, but each of their subjective experiences are equally qualified as true.

Unfortunately for universalists, a major logical problem invalidates this analogy. In the words of Matt Chandler, "The only way the parable of the Blind Men and the Elephant makes any sense is if the narrator of the story sees the whole elephant. The moment you claim ultimate reality is unknowable, you have just claimed the knowledge of what you said can't be known! This is intellectually inconsistent."

Seeking to validate their inconsistent beliefs, universalists hide under the guise of perennialism. Perennialism states that all religions share a single truth, that they may be superficially different on the outside, but they are inherently the same on the inside. Such a view is utterly false.

Too many doctrinal inconsistencies exist for all religions to be inherently the same. For example, the Bible claims Jesus is God's son, while the Quran says God cannot have a son. The Quran says that the righteous go to Paradise when they die, but Buddhism states that the righteous finally attain nirvana, where there is only oblivion. Thus, all religions may be superficially similar on the outside, but they are inherently *different* on the inside.

Dualism

Jesus' teaching, from the outset, was very dualistic. Jesus Himself said that "Whoever is not with me is against me, and whoever does not gather with me scatters" (Matt. 12:30). To Jesus it was this or that, Me or the world. There was no other option.

This reminds me of a story I once heard where Jesus and Satan were standing opposite each other, separated by a group of people in between them. They were selecting individuals from the group to join them. Thinking they had picked everybody, Jesus and Satan left with their followers, only to overlook one man. Absentmindedly swinging his legs back and forth, the man perched atop the fence erected between Jesus' territory and Satan's. It had not occurred to him to choose between the two. Not long after, however, he spotted Satan, who returned to the place and began to rove the area with his eyes.

"What are you looking for?" the man asked.

Spotting the man, Satan pointed at him. "You! You're coming with me!"

"But I didn't choose you," the man scowled, "or Jesus. I chose the fence."

A serene smile curled Satan's lips. "I own the fence."

Likewise, there are no neutral zones or spectator stands in life. Throughout His ministry, up until His very last meal, Jesus made it crystal clear that His message was either/or not both/and. He knew His message would bring division (Luke 12:51), and He required everyone to choose a side, take a stance. If you were not with Him, you were against Him. Satan owned the fence.

Inclusive Exclusivity

Does this mean that Jesus was hopelessly exclusive? Well, yes and no. Jesus' message of salvation was extremely exclusive to the extent that salvation could be found in no one but Himself. Yet He also taught that salvation was exceedingly inclusive in that it was open to everyone.

The Apostle John in Revelation records having seen the assembly of Heaven and hearing the choir sing to Jesus, "You are worthy to take the scroll and to open its seals, because you were slain, and with your blood you purchased for God persons from *every* tribe and language and people and nation" (Rev. 5:9) (emphasis added).

Jesus does not discriminate based on social, racial, or moral standing. Rather, He offers grace to all who repent and trust Him as their Lord and Savior. This did not sit well with many Jews in Jesus' day, as the Talmud (a collection of Jewish traditions) recorded that Jewish men prayed every morning, "I thank God that He did not make me a Gentile, He did not make me a woman, and He did not make me an ignoramus." Furthermore, orthodox Jews also prayed that there might be no Samaritans in the second resurrection. In other words, they degraded women and intellectually challenged people and prayed that all Samaritans might be sent to Hell.

Rather than pray these prayers, like the rest of His peers, Jesus went out of His way to minister to Samaritans, Gentiles, and women alike. To those whom others overlooked or undervalued, Jesus displayed the tender love of the Most High. This is why Timothy Keller said, "All religions are exclusive, but Christianity is the most inclusive exclusivity there is."

The Gospel of Jesus Christ is not limited to a select few, but rather it is the power of God that brings salvation to *all* who will believe (Rom. 1:16). Jesus did not shed His blood to save only a handful of people, but rather His atoning sacrifice enables multitudes of people to stand before God cleansed of their unrighteousness, redeemed in His sight.

Followers of the Way

In claiming He is the Way, Jesus illustrates that if His disciples want eternal life, they must enter through Him. He is the passageway to the Father. They cannot go around Him, they cannot go over Him, they must go through Him. In other words, even if an individual claims to believe in God, if he rejects Jesus, He has no hope of salvation.

So why is Jesus the way? Simply put, Jesus is the only way of salvation because of the will of the Father. It pleased the Father to make His Son the one and only way of salvation, for the ransom for sin required the life of a sinless person, and Jesus was the only one who could ever satisfy that debt. Not only is Jesus the way to salvation, He is also the way of fulfilling God's covenants, the way of overcoming sin and death, the way to blessing, and the way into Heaven.

Interestingly, early followers of Jesus became known as followers of "The Way" (Acts 24:24). Which way? The only way. Jesus did not claim to be *a* way, but *the* Way. The way is narrow. He taught: "Enter through the narrow gate. For wide is the gate and broad is the road that leads to destruction, and many enter through it. But small is the gate and narrow the road that leads to life, and only a few find it" (Matt. 7:13-14).

Unable to accept the exclusivity of Jesus' claim, many will instead choose to pursue so-called inclusive faiths, for Hell is all inclusive. The pit of destruction welcomes with open arms all beliefs and all walks of life, but the Kingdom of Heaven only admits genuine disciples of Jesus, followers of this beautiful Way.

Jesus made this way available through the purchase of His precious blood, a blood with which He ransomed all mankind so that He might restore His people unto Himself. If any other way could lead to Heaven, what would be the point of Jesus' suffering and death and resurrection? Jesus' priceless payment would be rendered worthless (Gal. 2:21).

Enter In

At this point, Jesus' teachings have come full circle. His first sermon, the Sermon on the Mount, depicted Him as the Way leading to life. Now His final sermon prior to His death did the same. How do you get to Heaven? Which way can I trust? Jesus' answer leaves no room for doubt.

He says in the Gospel of Matthew, "Enter through the narrow gate" (Matt. 7:13). Interestingly, the "invitation" Jesus offers to His crowd of listeners at the end of His sermon is nothing like the invitations we experience in today's churches. Nowhere does Jesus say, "Peter, begin to minister. Everyone bow your heads and close your eyes. If you have felt led at all during this time to ask me into your heart, just raise your hand. I see you, brother. Glory to God!"

No, instead, Jesus' invitation is a stern command. Enter through the narrow gate. He does not "suggest" entering. It is not enough to study the gate, to marvel over it, or to praise it. You must *enter* the gate! Jesus' command is not that of a tyrannical authoritarian, but rather the heartfelt cry of a loving father. It is our role to obey His command and heed His warning.

The necessity of trusting a loving father reminds me of a story I read years ago. On one occasion, a young boy was playing under a tree when he heard his father shout, "Son, keep your head down, and run to me!"

The boy hesitated. Why would his father disrupt his play-time? Yet, without opposition, he held his head down and ran towards his father.

Embracing his son, the boy's father pointed back to the tree, where an enormous snake began to crawl down the trunk. Had the boy not listened to his father's command, he would have suffered the snake's bite. The same is true for us. Disobeying Jesus' command leaves one vulnerable to the serpent's poison. Obeying it saves one's life.

Wide and Broad

Following His command, Jesus gives a warning. "For wide is the gate and broad is the road that leads to destruction, and many enter through it" (Matt. 7:13). First, the gate is wide, easy to find, and easy to enter in. Say this prayer, perform this sign, do this ritual, and you will be saved! Once you get past the wide gate, there is a broad way, with plenty of room for religious lollygagging. You can wander this way and that along the way without ever worrying about getting off the path. The broad road welcomes diverse doctrine and tolerance with no boundaries in sight, which lead only to division.

You can tread the path with other people, you can bring your baggage with you, and you can wander the road at the trajectory you deem fit. John MacArthur, in his sermon *Two Paths, One Way*, described the road in this way: "Bring your pride, bring your sin, bring your self-righteousness. No call for repentance. No commitment to a life of obedience to Christ. Just roll on with the crowd."

Furthermore, this wide gate and broad road is not marked "Hell." That would not sell well amongst the world populace.

Instead, modern culture teaches that all roads lead to Heaven, when in fact, only one gate and one narrow way leads to the blessed realm. Satan himself is responsible for reassigning the road markers, an act similar to that which the Hungarians committed against the Soviets. When the Soviet Union invaded Hungary, the Hungarians did not change the road signs. Instead, they changed the direction of the road markers. Satan does the same in our lives. He takes God's road marker and points it in the wrong direction.

"All are welcome!" he says. "There's plenty of room!" The Bible, however, teaches a much different truth. Psalm 1:6 says, "[T]he way of the wicked leads to destruction." Lots of men and women are out there selling tickets that they claim lead to Heaven, but these are tickets to Hell, fraudulently labeled "Heaven."

Small and Narrow

Unlike the wide gate and the broad way, Jesus says, "[S]mall is the gate and narrow the road that leads to life, and only a few find it" (Matt. 7:14). Not only is Jesus the Way, but He is also the Gate. In Jewish culture, a sheep pen did not have a wooden gate. Instead, the shepherd would lie down in the gate's entrance, so that no one could come in or out without his express permission. Jesus is the Good Shepherd, and no one joins or leaves His flock without going through Him.

Additionally, this gate is so small that to enter through it, you must lay aside your baggage. The way is so narrow that you cannot travel it with a group. It is like a turnstile, admitting only one person at a time. The broad way elevates group mentality, but the narrow way emphasizes the sobering truth that an individual is responsible for his faith and his alone. You must enter this gate unburdened, and you must enter it alone. In stark contrast to the broad road, the road of salvation is narrow. It is hemmed in all around by God's truth with no room whatsoever for leniency. Instead, there is a call for complete obedience to God's Word (Matt. 28:20).

Furthermore, unlike the other gate and the other way, only a few find the gate and road which lead to life. Knowing this, that few would find Him, Jesus said in the Gospel of Luke, "Make *every* effort to enter through the narrow door, because *many*, I tell you, will try to enter and will not be able to" (Luke 13:24) (added emphasis). "Strive!" Jesus commands. "Fight the good fight!" Do not lollygag, compromise, or slumber, but strive, making every effort to enter through the narrow gate!

Jeff O'Hara, in his poem *Blame Me Not*, put it this way:

> Why call Me Lord, Lord and do not the things I say? You call me the way, and walk me not? You call me the life, and live me not? You call me Master, and obey me not? If I condemn you, blame me not. You call me bread, and eat me not? You call me truth, and believe me not? You call me Lord, and serve me not. If I condemn you, blame me not!

Jesus promises that those who enter through this gate and tread this narrow path will reach their destination: life. Following Jesus has its benefits. We do not follow Him only to perish. Rather, we follow Him knowing that He leads us to a life of purpose and glory.

Losing the Path

In the blockbuster film *The Hobbit: The Desolation of Smaug*, the wizard Gandalf leads Bilbo Baggins and the company of thirteen dwarves to the enchanted forest of Mirkwood. The only way to safely pass through the forest is by remaining on the winding, stone path. Gandalf warned, "Cross only by the stone bridge. The very air in the forest is heavy with illusion. It will seek to enter your mind and lead you astray. You must stay on the path. Do not leave it. If you do, you will never find it again. No matter what may come, stay on the path."

For a long while, the dwarves manage with difficulty to do just this, but as the forest's enchantment settles on them, they begin to lose their way. At length, the company comes to an abrupt halt, leading the dwarf leader to ask another dwarf why they have stopped. Pointing to the imminent cliff, the dwarf answers, "The path, it's disappeared!"

"What's going on?" another dwarf asks.

A fourth dwarf utters in horror: "We've lost the path!"

This is exactly what Jesus warned. Do not stray from the narrow way. Strive to stay on the path, for if you lose it, you may never find it again. Thus, the root problem in American society is this: we've lost the path. We've lost our way. Instead, we have been led astray by sinful illusions, wandering headlong in the direction of an imminent cliff. Will America ever find the path again? Only God knows. Only God knows.

Conclusion

The centrality and exclusivity of Jesus is one of the most despised doctrines among secular circles. Christians who uphold these truths will often find themselves under attack. This is what happened to Russell Vought when he appeared before a committee as President Trump's nominee for Deputy Director of the Office of Budget and Management.

Bernie Sanders, an orthodox Jew, accused Russell Vought of prejudice when Vought wrote this statement: "Muslims do not simply have a deficient theology. They do not know God because they have rejected Jesus Christ His Son, and they stand condemned."

After a slew of personal diatribes aimed at Vought's religious convictions, Sanders asked, "In your judgment, do you think that people who are not Christians are going to be condemned?"

Vought answered, "As a Christian, I believe that all individuals are made in the image of God and are worthy of dignity and respect, regardless of their religious beliefs." Vought added, "I believe that as a Christian, that's how I should treat all individuals—"

To which Sanders interrupted, "And do you think your statement that you put in that publication, 'They do not know God because they rejected Jesus Christ the Son, and they stand condemned,' do you think that's respectful of other religions?"

While it is possible to respect other people without consenting to the veracity of their religious claims, Sanders and others like him are not fools. They realize that, in the end, Christianity and its founder, Jesus, claim that adherents to any other religion cannot experience a relationship with God. These critics bypass the completely inclusive nature of Jesus' invitation to follow Him and instead stumble on the notion that without following Him they are lost.

Regardless of our beliefs or practices, each of us one day will stand before the Almighty. In a way, all religions do end up at the same place: the judgment seat of God. Only one faith, though, holds the answer as to how an individual can stand before God in a favorable light. Only one Way, that of Jesus, will allow us to stand before God acquitted of our sin. Jesus did not come to Earth to act as a way-shower, rather, He came to identify Himself as *the one and only Way* to the Father. Choose Him, and live, or oppose Him, and perish (John 3:18). God's vantage point offers no neutral position.

PART FOUR

Exit: The Way Is Completed

XIV: THE SUFFERING SERVANT

Date: c. AD 30
Location: Jerusalem's Upper City

Blood and sweat blurred Jesus' vision as He stumbled forward, the weight of the crossbeam bearing down on His shoulders. In years past, Jesus had constructed these very beams, thus, the feel of one was not unfamiliar, but the circumstances were. Just as Isaac, the son of Abraham, bore the wood for his sacrifice in compliance with his father's command, so Jesus bore the cross-beam for His own sacrifice, as His Father had instructed.

After three years of healing and ministering, Jesus was repaid for His loving kindness by a bitter betrayal, a rigged trial, and a cruel sentence. The Jewish authorities, despising Jesus' growing fame, conspired against Him, and with the aid of one of Jesus' own apostles, they arrested Jesus and brought Him before the Roman magistrate, Pontius Pilate.

Pilate initially sought to free Jesus, but he ultimately bowed to pressure, handing Jesus over to the executioners. Jesus' crime? Claiming to be King of the Jews, a title only Rome could grant.

Horrifically scourged for the viewing pleasure of Jews and Romans alike, Jesus endured the pain in accordance with the will of His Father. This was the way, ordained before the foundation of the world, by which mankind would be reconciled to God.

Failure?

By worldly standards, Jesus' life appeared to be that of a failure. He was unmarried with no children to carry on His family lineage, His own family disbelieved His message (John 7:5), one of His closest friends betrayed Him (Matt. 26:14), His people condemned Him (Matt. 26:66), and God seemingly forsook Him (Matt. 27:46). While His life on Earth did include times of great joy, He was often a man of many sorrows, tired, hungry, and grieved. His life was bereft of material comfort, and He owned nothing for which others might esteem Him. Rather, everything He had was borrowed: His food, His housing, even His transportation. He said of Himself, "Foxes have dens and birds have nests, but the Son of Man has no place to lay his head" (Matt. 8:20).

Jesus was tempted in every way, yet without sin. Even so, the anguish of His spirit climaxed the night of His arrest, one day prior to His execution. Having led His apostles from the city where they had eaten together, Jesus brought them to the Garden of Gethsemane.

Pressed

The Garden of Gethsemane lay at the foot of the Mount of Olives, famous for its olive groves. Gethsemane in Greek means "oil press," for it was here that olives were harvested and pressed for use. Ironically, it was here also that Jesus, the Messiah (or "Anointed One"), was pressed. Yet, when He was pressed, it was not oil but blood that dripped out (Luke 22:44). Scholars identify this very rare medical condition as hematidrosis, wherein an extreme level of anxiety will cause a person's capillaries to burst. Why was Jesus so hard-pressed?

Jesus had told His disciples, "My soul is overwhelmed with sorrow to the point of death" (Mark 14:34). This sorrow was on account of the vision He had received moments prior (Mark 14:33). All in a moment, the Father revealed to Jesus the imminent judgment for humanity' sin that He was about to endure. The Bible summarizes Jesus' reaction to this vision by saying only two things: He was greatly distressed; and He was troubled.

To say Jesus was greatly distressed would be an understatement. When He tells His disciples that His pain is such that He might prematurely die, He is not exaggerating (Mark 14:34). Additionally, the Greek meaning for the word "troubled" means to be overcome with shocking horror. This would be the feeling you would experience if you came home one day only to find your family murdered and blood everywhere. Jesus beheld this horrible murder, He beheld the dark stains of blood, but it was His murder and His blood!

Upon beholding this vision, Jesus responded in a manner unlike every Hollywood hero. "'Abba, Father,' he said, 'everything is possible for you. Take this cup from me. Yet not what I will, but what you will'" (Mark 14:36). What? When pressed, William Wallace of *Braveheart* yelled, "Freedom!" When pressed, Captain America taunted, "I can do this all day!" But, when pressed, Jesus sought a way out—not just once, but three times!

When the Father does not grant Jesus' first request, Jesus leaves only to come back to His prayer spot and ask again, "My Father, if it is not possible for this cup to be taken away unless I drink it, may your will be done" (Matt. 26:42).

What is this cup that Jesus keeps mentioning? Isaiah refers to God's wrath against humanity's sins as a cup (Is. 51:17). So, the cup Jesus was to drink was not just physical torture, but His Father's wrath against the sin of the world. Furthermore, in Jewish culture, as part of the wedding ritual, the husband would drink from a cup as a sign that he would lay down his life for his bride. Jesus, in a sense, wondered if the marriage could be called off. He was having second thoughts. Was the bride really worth all the trouble?

It is in this moment that the humanity of Jesus is clearest seen, almost even dominating His divinity. During this hour, Jesus expresses what every human being feels in the face of pain and suffering: loneliness and fear. His divinity was willing, but His humanity, His flesh, was hesitant (Matt. 26:41).

"If it's possible," Jesus prayed, "if there's any other way, if there's any other substitute, Father, take this cup from me!" Yet, in Jesus' darkest hour, in the midst of His suffering, He did not forget *who* He was or *whose* He was. Each time He prayed for the Father to remove the cup, He always said, "Yet, not what I will, but what you will!"

Jesus prayed this prayer three times, but after three times, the Father's answer remained the same. His answer was complete and firm: there was no other way. Jesus was the only substitute able to bear sin's burden (Acts 4:12). So, why did the Father subject Jesus to the torment of this vision? Johnathan Edwards, in his sermon *Christ's Agony*, put it this way: "Christ, as God, perfectly knew what these sufferings were; but it was more needful also that he should know as man; for he was to suffer as man, and the act of Christ in taking that cup was the act of Christ as God man." In other words, Jesus received this vision so that we could understand His choice to sacrificially die was voluntary. Cosigned to obedience, Jesus overcame the weakness of the flush and echoed the battle cry of every born-again believer. "Not my will, O God, but yours be done!"

Jesus in My Place

Shortly after His garden suffering, Jesus was arrested, subjected to a sham trial, and passed on to Pilate. When Pilate received Him, however, He found no reason to punish Him. Jesus did not merit so much as a slap on the wrist! Yet the Jewish leaders demanded He be crucified. To appease the rowdy crowd, Pilate brought Jesus out with a murderer named Barabbas. It was Pilate's custom during Jewish Passover to release to the Jews a prisoner of their choosing, and so, Pilate hoped that the Jewish populace would drown out the objections of the Jewish leaders and choose to free Jesus. Such was not the case.

Instead, like vipers, the Pharisees moved amongst the people calling for them to demand Jesus' crucifixion. Mark 15:11 says, "But the chief priests stirred up the crowd to have Pilate release Barabbas instead." Satan knows how to move a crowd. He knows how to get the crowd on his side. He will use fear, charisma, subtlety, whatever it takes to stir a crowd. Thus, the ambassadors of Satan whipped the crowd into a frenzy, calling for Barabbas' release and Jesus' death. It was not enough that Jesus had already been beaten and humiliated. The Jewish leaders wanted

Him dead! Never before had such an innocent person faced such unjust punishment, yet Jesus did it willingly.

Even moments before His death, He was illustrating His substitutionary role by taking Barabbas' place. Barabbas, a sinful rebel, symbolized the human race. Yet Jesus, innocent and holy, took His place.

Thus, the Gospel, the Good News, is this: Jesus in my place (Rom. 3:25; Matt. 20:28; 2 Cor. 5:21). Did Jesus deserve to die? No. Did I? Yes. "[H]e was pierced for our transgressions, he was crushed for our iniquities; the punishment that brought us peace was on him, and by his wounds we are healed" (Is. 53:5). Jesus suffered and died in my place so that I might live.

A Public Spectacle

Following Jesus' sentencing, Pilate gave Jesus over to the executioners. Prior to His crucifixion, however, Jesus was forced to undergo further humiliation. According to Roman practice, the Romans would parade convicted criminals in the streets before the populace to show the consequences of opposing Roman law. In this manner, the Romans hoped to quell any rebellious thoughts among the people by having them look upon the brutal fate of those who attempted to subvert Roman rule.

Thus, Jesus was dragged through the winding streets of Jerusalem along the path infamously known as the Via Dolorosa, the Way of Suffering. All the while, He bore around His neck a plaque displaying His charge, "King of the Jews," and across His shoulders a weighty cross beam. The cross' main stake lay in waiting for Jesus at Golgotha, just outside Jerusalem, but Jesus was forced to bear the burden of His own means of execution.

Becoming Sin

Not only was Jesus called to bear a physical burden, that of the cross beam, but His primary task was to bear an even greater spiritual pain, that of the crushing weight of sin. By all standards, the burden of sin far outweighed that of the cross beam He hauled on His shoulders.

On that cruel day, later known as Good Friday, Jesus felt the weight of all humanity's sin piled upon Him. The Apostle Paul would later write that "God made him who had no sin to be *sin* for us, so that in Him we might become the righteousness of God" (2 Cor. 5:21) (emphasis added).

The Scripture here uses the Hebrew word *chatta'ath*, which means both sin and sin offering. Thus, Jesus became sin judicially not actually. God treated Him as sin, yet Jesus was unblemished, like the Passover Lamb. It was no coincidence that Jesus was killed during Passover season, for He came to fulfill the Scriptures. In the origin of Passover, God commanded the Israelites, through Moses, to kill a spotless lamb and spread its blood across the doorposts of their homes. Only then would death pass over them. In the same way, Jesus, the spotless Lamb of God (1 Peter 1:19), was sacrificed during Passover, His blood spread across a wood frame that all those who took shelter in Him might escape death's cruel grip.

When Jesus voluntarily became our sin offering, He took upon Himself the enormity of God's wrath. The sin of the world covered Jesus, but it did not become Him. Jesus remained pure, much to the disdain of Satan and his allies. Just as the thorns in Genesis 3 represented the curse of sin, so did the crown of thorns thrust upon Christ's head. As sin's embodiment, Christ wore its symbol (Matt. 27:29).

Outside the City

Jewish law required that executions be performed outside Jerusalem, the Holy City, in accordance with the Law of Moses (Num. 15:35). To appease the Jewish populace, the Romans consented to their custom and executed crucifixion outside the city limits. Taking Jesus to the appointed place of crucifixion, the Romans unwittingly underscored the wisdom and plan of God.

While on Earth, Jesus rejected the modern teachings of the Pharisees. The Jewish religious teachers had corrupted the laws and ordinances of God and focused on the rituals rather than the heart. Therefore, Jesus displayed His separation from the teachers and their practices by keeping Himself apart from them. Even in death, Jesus displayed that He was outside their realm of anthropocentric beliefs.

Notably, Jewish law dictated that most sacrifices could be offered only in the Temple, and that God would not look upon the sacrifice offered by those who violated this law. One exception existed, though: that of a sin offering. A sin offering constituted an unblemished animal, whose blood remedied unintentional sins. Only sin offerings were made outside the city. Fittingly, Jesus, the perfect offering for mankind's sins, was sacrificed outside the Holy City; His blood shed to atone for the sins of formerly blinded sinners.

Jesus' contemporaries failed to recognize not only the practice of a sin offering as foreshadowing Jesus' ultimate sacrifice, they also overlooked the significance of the Jewish practice of a scapegoat. The Law of Moses dictated that a pair of goats would be selected, one of which would be sacrificed, and the other (the scapegoat) which would be released into the wilderness. The high priest would do as follows:

[He would] lay both hands on the head of the live goat and confess over it all the wickedness and rebellion of the Israelites—all their sins—and put them on the goat's head. He shall send the goat away into the wilderness in the care of someone appointed for the task. The goat will carry on itself all their sins to a remote place; and the man shall release it in the wilderness.

Leviticus 16:21-22

Jesus was our scapegoat. He was taken outside of the city to a barren place so that He might bear the iniquities of all people. While most Jews believed the scapegoat wandered free, Jewish priests ensured that a man standing by would take the goat and throw it over a cliff to protect the people from the ill omen of the scapegoat wandering back into the camp. Likewise, Jesus faced the cliff each one of us is bound to face, that of death, but He faced it once for us all. He took the plunge, bearing our iniquities, that He might rid His people of their sin.

Joy in the Midst of Suffering

Jesus was not looking for a way out of the crucifixion. He did not attempt to make a run for it, He did not try to incite His followers against His captors, nor did He request His Father to dispatch a contingent of heavenly angels. Rather, with the greatest restraint known to the universe, Jesus resisted the physical urge to seek a way out of the pain and pressed onward.

Why did Jesus go through with His execution? How was He able to do so?

The writer of Hebrews answers this question with a remarkable statement. "For the joy set before him he endured the cross, scorning its shame, and sat down at the right hand of the throne of God" (Heb. 12:2).

What got Jesus through that dreadful hour? It was the joy He had knowing that the hour was near when humanity, His most beloved creation, would at long last be reconciled unto Himself. The tears He shed were not only tears of pain, but also tears of joy. This day was one long waited for by both prophets and Jesus Himself. Now, it finally came to pass. Thus, with insurmountable confidence, one that Satan and all the demons of Hell could not quench, Jesus persevered towards the place of His crucifixion.

Jesus was about to fulfill the role for which He was born. The King of Heaven, to whom all nations and peoples will bow, endured unimaginable shame and pain, declaring it all worth the joy that would result from His sacrifice.

The Way to Heaven that Jesus professed to His listeners throughout His ministry was coming to fruition. Jesus was the Way, the appointed sacrifice, and within a few torturous hours, the gates to Heaven would be opened at last, accessible to the very last of Christ's servants. Perceiving the closed gates, Jesus pressed on towards the hour when the gates would open, never to close again.

Conclusion

There are a growing number of people today who despise the doctrine of penal substitutionary atonement. Some say that it maligns the character of God as that of a cosmic child abuser, but these proponents fail to understand the Triune nature of God. Jesus was no less God than the Father, and Jesus Himself said this: "The reason my Father loves me is that I lay down my life—only to take it up again" (John 10:17). Jesus voluntarily suffered and died, but again, people such as

Steve Chalke protest, "Why can't God do what He asked us to do 'freely forgive without demanding retribution first'?"

The writer of the Epistle to the Hebrews said it this way: "In fact, the law requires that nearly everything be cleansed with blood, and without the shedding of blood there is no forgiveness" (Heb. 9:22). Forgiveness is not free. It comes at a price. Even in the parable of the Prodigal Son, where some like to argue that no payment was required for forgiveness, the father was forced to incur his son's debts. He bore the consequences of his son's actions upon himself. Likewise, God bore our sin and shame upon Himself that we might be forgiven.

Todd White and others say, "The cross to me isn't a revelation of my sin. The cross is actually the revealing of my value." That is not what the Bible says. Instead, the Bible teaches emphatically that "while we were still sinners, Christ died for us" (Rom. 5:8). He did not die for us when we were in a purely righteous state; He died for us while we were still opposed to Him! Paul Washer said it best. "People say 'the cross is a sign of how much man is worth!' That's not true! The cross is a sign of how depraved we really are – that it took the death of God's own Son!"

One of the most frequently asked theological questions involves the problem of suffering. Why do we suffer? If God is all-powerful, all-good, and all-knowing, then why do we suffer? Would He not want to end suffering? No other religion ever truly solves the problem of evil or suffering. The Hindus believe suffering is part of life's balance, the Buddhists believe it is all an illusion, the Muslims say that suffering and evil are part of Allah's will, but Christianity takes evil and suffering upon itself in the form of Jesus Christ. When Jesus hangs on the cross, we see that suffering is not limited to humanity, but God Himself suffered. Thus, when people ask, "Why do bad things happen to good people," we know that it only ever happened once, and He volunteered.

XV: IT IS FINISHED

Date: c. AD 30
Location: Golgotha outside Jerusalem

Upon reaching Golgotha, the place of the skull, Jesus was offered sour wine mixed with gall to numb the pain. After tasting it, Jesus refused to drink further. His time had come.

Soldiers methodically positioned Him onto the cross, stretching out His arms and overlapping His feet. Drawing deep breaths, He prepared for the inevitable. He felt the pointed nail pressed against His wrist, followed by the swift, harsh stroke of the hammer ripping the nail through His flesh.

Screeching in pain, Jesus coughed up blood as His eyes began to tear up. Again and again the hammer swung until all three nails had been firmly implanted through His wrists and feet.

Jesus burst into tears from the excruciating pain as the Roman soldiers tugged on the ropes that secured the beam, raising His cross to stand high in the air as the beam sank into a prepared hole deep in the ground. So it was that the King of Heaven, He whom Isaiah saw high and lifted up, was suspended in mockery above the Earth.

He was held captive between Heaven and Earth by His obedience, unable to leave Earth and unable to reach Heaven until His Father's command. He was trapped in the middle. He resembled the Israelites, who were caught between the walls of the Red Sea. In front of them lay the Promised Land; behind them was the Egyptian Army.

He had experienced betrayal, suffered scorn, and now, He would endure the cross.

Why Crucifixion?

Crucifixion was a painfully cruel way to die. Adopted from the Persians, the Romans used crucifixion as a form of capital punishment, reserving it for only the worst criminals. This method of execution was purposefully slow and torturous.

The crucified individual would have nails driven through his wrists to secure them to a wooden beam so that his torso would not slump forward. Another nail was pierced through his overlapping feet to ensure he remained suspended without the weight of his body causing the nails to rip through his wrists. Fastened to the cross, he would attempt to lift himself upward on a small stool to gasp for breath. Each time he drew himself up, the nail driven between his two feet would tear deeper into his flesh. All the while, the blood in his lungs would clog his windpipe, causing the victim to slowly asphyxiate. In the case of Jesus, He was deprived of a stool, for Passover was near and the Jews wanted Him dead before then. Thus, the pain of suffocation was even more agonizing in His circumstance.

Why would our Savior subject Himself to such cruelty? Surely, a more humane death would have sufficed. Why could He not simply have fallen asleep or consumed a quick-acting poison? Why did He allow Himself to suffer so?

By His crucifixion, Jesus was fulfilling prophecy. But, since He is God, one could argue that Jesus could have prophesied that He would die by falling asleep or by some other less painful death. Yet, prophecy declared that He must be crucified. Why?

First the punishment for sin is death. Thus, Jesus had to die if He were to take the punishment for our sin. Second, the Bible teaches that the life of an individual is in His blood (Lev. 17:11). Thus, Jesus had to suffer a bloody death. Third, sin was a capital offense against God. And Jesus took on the sin of the world. Thus, Jesus underwent crucifixion, which was the most brutal, highest form of capital punishment in His day. Finally, Jesus' harsh form of death allowed Him to become so intimately acquainted with affliction that we know He can sympathize with us in ours (Heb. 4:15).

Thus, Jesus submitted Himself under His Father's yoke and underwent the excruciating pain of the cross. Crucifixion usually lasted between eighteen to forty-eight hours, but such was the pain Jesus experienced (compounded by the prior flogging, beatings, and lack of sleep) that He was dead within six hours.

The Will of the Father and Son

During the course of Jesus' crucifixion, He experienced the mockery of both physical and spiritual enemies. Onlookers and passers-by alike scorned Him saying, "He saved others; let him save himself, if he is the Christ of God, his Chosen One!" (Luke 23:35).

The Pharisees and Roman soldiers joined in the mockery, with the Pharisees going so far as to say, "He saved others; he cannot save himself. He is the King of Israel; let him come down now from the cross, and we will believe in him" (Matt. 27:42).

While to others, Jesus' exposed body made Him appear vulnerable, Jesus was by no means weak. He could have easily called upon His Father to dispatch a regiment of angels, thus abandoning the plan to redeem humanity. After all, despite His years of ministry and the many signs and wonders He performed, they still did not believe.

In wrath, for the blatant blasphemy spoken against God and the utter disbelief of the people, Jesus could have descended from the cross and ushered in the judgment of the nations, but He did not. He attempted once to escape the cross, by means of petition, but after receiving the Father's resolute answer, Jesus resolved to submit entirely to the Father's will

To those watching, it appeared that the nails were keeping Jesus on the cross, but that was not so. Jesus' will was the only power keeping Him on the cross that day, and while the flesh was weak, His will was strong! Despite the petty words of others, despite their arrogance and disbelief, Jesus refused to come down. He descended once out of obedience, from Heaven, but He would not descend again, from the cross, without the explicit command of His Father. This was the will of God.

The Impenitent Thief

At this time, one of the thieves crucified besides Jesus cried out, "Aren't you the Messiah? Save yourself!" (Luke 23:39).

This statement came both as a mockery and a temptation. On the thief's part, he meant to scorn Jesus, joining in the crowd mentality. In his suffering, he accused a righteous man, much like Job's wife who called on the pious Job to curse God and die. However, Jesus showed even greater piety than Job by refusing to answer the words of a fool and the temptation of Satan.

While on the surface, the thief's words seemed simply aimed to mock Jesus, Jesus understood that the thief was being used by the devil to tempt Jesus away from His calling. If Satan could somehow manage to get Jesus off the cross, he would succeed in finally driving a permanent wedge between God and mankind. Satan had no power in and of himself to remove Jesus, thus, he had to get Jesus to choose to remove Himself!

Unmoved by the devil's attempt, Jesus held fast to the purpose of God. Yet, even as the cry of enemies echoed all around Jesus, a stranger suddenly spoke out in His defense.

The Penitent Thief

The other thief opposite Jesus (often referred to as Dismas) rallied to Jesus' defense. "Don't you fear God," he said, "since you are under the same sentence? We are punished justly, for we are getting what our deeds deserve. But this man has done nothing wrong" (Luke 23:40-41).

The Bible does not give us much information regarding the penitent thief, but what we do know is that he is a criminal condemned to death, and that it "just so happened" that He was crucified with Jesus. If life is clear about anything, it is that there is no such thing as a coincidence. By dying alongside the two thieves, Jesus offered them one last chance to receive salvation before they perished. The first thief refused the offer, having come face-to-face with His Savior and choosing instead to mock Him. The second thief, however, was a different story.

The second thief recognized two things.

First, he acknowledged his own depravity, that he was a sinner, justified in his condemnation. The thief was deserving of punishment, as all sinners are. It is interesting how some people view this passage and remark how crucifixion for thievery is simply too harsh. The reality, though, is that any grievance against God's law, no matter how small, is deserving of death. However, there is hope. Second, the penitent thief confessed the righteousness of Christ. Christ was blameless in God's eyes, the spotless sacrificial lamb, the only one able to pay the ultimate price. He was crushed for our iniquities, but He Himself was without sin. While the religious leaders, those who claimed to know what perfection looked like, accused Jesus of blasphemy, heresy, demon-possession, and other manners of uncleanliness, the sinful, condemned thief on the cross declared Jesus to be innocent, free from all wrong.

Thus, in that moment at Calvary, God did not use a preacher, but a thief to proclaim His truth. God showed with Balaam, centuries prior, His willingness to use even a donkey, rather than a prophet, to speak on His behalf, and here again, God shows that He is able to use any instrument, no matter how lowly, for His purpose.

Upon the thief's confession of Jesus' purity, He went a step further. He could have stopped there, but there was one last thing to say, a petition. He boldly requested, "Jesus, remember me when you come into your kingdom" (Luke 23:42).

What a profession! While others saw a cross, the penitent thief saw a throne. Others saw Jesus as a criminal, but the thief saw Him as the one true King. His plea was earnest, the cry of one desperate, yet hopeful.

Who knows how much he knew concerning Jesus? No doubt he might have heard all kinds of stories, but on the last day of his life, the thief chose to stop stealing, and start seeking. Heaven could not be stolen. It had to be sought after. Thus, the penitent thief made a solemn request, one that no individual ever asked of Jesus: that Jesus remember him when Jesus entered His kingdom.

The rich young ruler asked Jesus how he could receive eternal life, Nicodemus inquired as to the nature of Jesus' ministry, but no one ever simply, boldly requested that Jesus remember that individual when He entered Heaven. It was a genuine, audacious request, one which Jesus acquiesced to immediately.

"Truly I tell you, today you will be with me in paradise" (Luke 23:43). Even moments before His death, Jesus was still transforming lives. While He was losing His life, He was still saving the lives of others. Hallelujah!

My God, My God

Following Jesus' declaration to the penitent thief, the Bible says that "From noon until three in the afternoon darkness came over all the land" (Matt. 27:45).

This was a physical sign from Creation that the created order objected to the suffering of the Creator. Jesus Himself said that should men stop praising Him, the rocks would cry out

(Luke 19:40). Thus, when the penitent thief finally fell silent, and the enemies of Christ rallied against Him, nature spoke on Jesus' behalf. At a time of day when the sun should have shown brightest, the skies dimmed, protesting Jesus' death. While usually nature is indifferent to the suffering of man, the sun shining while wars rage, the birds chirping while funerals proceed, such was not the case the day Jesus was crucified.

Still, those watching remained stubborn. Jesus found it easier to calm the raging seas than to appeal to the unbelief of so many men and women. However, while Jesus was able to cope with the scorn of men, something shifted upon the presence of darkness that caused Him to waver. It was not the absence of physical light, but rather, the presence of God's spiritual light dimmed in that moment.

Unable to look upon Jesus, who in that moment took upon Himself the sin of the world, the Father looked away. Every good parent knows never to look away from their child, so how is it that the good, good Father of our Lord Jesus looked away from His Son at the moment of Jesus' greatest peril?

God is not famous for His explicit answers to our pressing questions, but what He is known for is answering the underlying, unasked questions. When Jesus said, *"Eli, Eli, lema sabachthani?"* (which means "My God, my God, why have you forsaken me?") (Matt. 27:46), He was drawing attention to Psalm 22.

In this Messianic Psalm, David prophesied the suffering of God's Chosen One in vivid description that matched up perfectly with Jesus' current circumstances. In referencing this Scripture, Jesus hoped to bring to light once more, through the words of Scripture, the purpose for His current trials. He attempted to enlighten those around Him to the fact that He was fulfilling prophecy before their very eyes: their Messiah had come!

Simultaneously, His utterance demonstrated that Jesus experienced actual, momentary separation from God's presence. This is a phenomenon beyond phenomenon. How can God experience separation from Himself? How can the perfect Father turn away from the perfect Son? We may not receive the answer to the question of Jesus' suffering, but because of this situation, we do receive the answer to our own suffering.

Jesus was able to sympathize with our weakness by petitioning God in His hour of need. Thus, we have assurance that there is no greater, impartial mediator than He who empathized with our every plight. He was forgotten so that through grace those who believe in Him might never be.

I Thirst

At long last, Jesus' hour had come. The flesh grew weaker and weaker with every excruciating passing second, but the Spirit inside of Him experienced greater longing. Jesus' spirit desired nothing more than finally to leave His fleshly body and to be restored to the Father in Heaven. Before He could die, though, Jesus had one last thing to say.

The Apostle John who witnessed this miraculous event recorded, "After this." After His scourgings, after the mockeries He endured, after His friends abandoned Him, after His own Father turned away from Him. "After this, Jesus, knowing that all was now finished, said (to fulfill the Scripture), 'I thirst'" (John 19:28, ESV).

John used the parentheses because, at the time, He did not understand that this was what was taking place. That is how it is in our own lives. Sometimes we have to live between the parentheses, not knowing that our current situation plays a part in the grand scheme of God's narrative. In these spaces, it is essential to meditate on God's purpose and provision, even if we seem forsaken.

Thus, as Jesus hung on the cross, He rested in the confidence that He had finished not just *some* things, or even *most* things. He had now finished *everything*! His death would not be sufficient just for a select few or a majority. Instead, it would prove utterly sufficient for everyone who called on His Name.

I cannot imagine the thoughts coursing through Jesus' head as He realized at last that everything was finished. The pain in His body was unbearable, but upon realizing His time was at hand, Jesus felt an insurmountable joy rise up inside Him. The hour had come at last, the hour long looked for and even longer hoped for. No longer did Jesus need to suffer. No longer did humanity need to suffer, for all things were now finished. The Scriptures were fulfilled.

Thus, Jesus summoned what little breath He had remaining and made a request. "I am thirsty" (John 19:28).

He who spoke the waters into existence, He who called Himself "Living Water," the very fount of salvation, thirsted. The fount of all springs thirsted! Each one of us are thirsty, seeking that which will not satisfy, but on the cross, Jesus thirsted so that you and I would never have to! He was not thirsty for what the world had to offer (Mark 15:23), but only for that which enabled Him to fulfill His Father's purpose.

In response to Jesus' request, the Roman guards noticed "[a] jar of wine vinegar was there, so they soaked a sponge in it, put the sponge on a stalk of the hyssop plant, and lifted it to Jesus' lips" (John 19:29).

Drinking from the sponge, Jesus took a deep breath and prepared for the big finish.

Tetelestai

Upon receiving the drink, Jesus looked up to Heaven with blood-stained, swollen eyes. In the English language, Jesus pronounced three simple words, "It is finished" (John 19:30).

Those mocking Jesus believed this to be a sign that He finally abandoned His masquerade and acknowledged His defeat. However, Jesus' statement had much more powerful implications.

His statement becomes clearer when translated into the Greek. The Greek word used here is *tetelestai*. *Tetelestai* has double meanings in Greek and ancient culture.

The first meaning is "it is paid in full." In Greek culture, when an individual paid off his debts, the lender would stamp the contract with the word *tetelestai*. It is paid in full.

In the same way, Christ took our contract and stamped in blood the word *tetelestai*. It is paid in full. His blood fully satisfied our debt. The power of sin was great, requiring nothing less than the blood of the very Creator to satisfy it, but this did not hinder Christ. He paid our debt in full, cancelling out our record of wrong. We are no longer in debt to sin, but rather, we have been set free from it, for He is both the one who made the payment and the one to whom the payment was owed. Hence, He is the only one authorized to declare, *"Tetelestai!"*

The second meaning of *tetelestai* is the more commonly used phrase "it is finished." In ancient culture, when a painter completed the last stroke of his masterpiece, he declared, *"Tete-*

lestai!" When a builder placed the last brick on his building, he exclaimed, "*Tetelestai!*"

In this context, *tetelestai* represented the last action in a master plan. The plan of salvation was long in the making, extending all the way back to the Garden of Eden (Genesis 3:15). Thus, when Jesus cried His last words, He was indeed fulfilling the final step in the greatest of all master plans.

Paradidomi

With His last dying breath, "Jesus called out with a loud voice, 'Father, into your hands I commit my spirit.' When he had said this, he breathed his last" (Luke 23:46). The Hebrew word for commit is *paradidomi*. *Paradidomi* can mean betray, commit, deliver, or hand over. Thus, the Gospel writers record how Jesus, the innocent Son of God was handed over by sinners, but in His last hour, we see Jesus hand over His spirit to God.

While it may have appeared to have been Judas who handed over Jesus to the Jews (Matt. 26:15), or Caiaphas who handed over Jesus to the Romans (Matt. 27:2), or Pilate who handed over Jesus to the executioners (Matt. 27:26), God was actually the One doing the handing over (Acts 2:23). Jesus Himself declared that no one takes His life. He lays it down. *Paradidomi!* He handed it over! For what reason did He hand over His life? So that what was taken from Him might be restored, handed over, to Him.

Earlier in the Gospel of Luke when Jesus was tempted in the wilderness, Satan boasted, "I will give You all this realm and its glory [its power, its renown]; because it has been *handed over* to me, and I give it to whomever I wish" (Luke 4:6, AMP) (emphasis added). God gave stewardship of the earth to Adam, but Adam forfeited the keys to Satan. Yet, upon Jesus' death, Jesus confronted the devil asking, "What's that you're holding?"

"Oh, this?" the devil indicated one key on his keychain. "This is the key to death."

His arms outstretched, Jesus thundered, "All authority in heaven and on earth has been handed over to me! I dealt with death, so *paradidomi*! Hand it over!"

The devil sheepishly removed the key from his keychain whilst attempting to hide his remaining key.

"What's that?" Jesus pointed to the other key.

"That? Oh, that's just the key to Hades and eternal suffering."

"Well, I dealt with that too, so hand it over!"

All the power of the enemy has been handed over to Him who was dead but reigns forevermore. Yet, the devil is not the only one commanded to hand over his possessions to Jesus. "What is it you're holding onto?" Jesus asks us. "Sin? I paid for that. *Paradidomi*! Shame? I was despised and rejected so that you wouldn't have to be. *Paradidomi*! Hand it over." Unless we hand over to Him all that hinders us from surrendering to Him, He cannot hand over to us the gift of salvation that was purchased with His blood. Thus, I earnestly beg you, *Paradidomi*! Hand it over and praise God that the hand that once held doesn't hold you anymore, for "if the Son has set you free, you will be free indeed" (John 8:36).

Conclusion

Years following the crucifixion, Christians would be scorned and mocked for putting their faith in a crucified criminal. Yet Jesus had warned them that this would be so. The word "excruciating" itself comes from a Latin word, *ex* meaning intense, and *crux* meaning cross. Ironically, only two centuries later, the cross would stand not for defeat but for victory under the reign of Roman Emperor Constantine.

Unfortunately, today, we have all but forgotten the message of the cross. We have reduced the cross to a piece of jewelry we wear around our neck, or a tattoo that adorns our skin. But the cross of Jesus Christ is the heart of the Gospel. It is "a stumbling block to Jews and foolishness to Gentiles, but to those whom God has called, both Jews and Greeks, [it is] Christ the power of God and the wisdom of God" (1 Cor. 1:22-24). The cross is Jesus, His arms outstretched, proclaiming that He has prepared the way for us to eternal life.

On a tree was hung the fruit that led to death, of which Adam and Eve ate, and also on a tree was hung the fruit that leads to life, the apple of God's eye. Those who eat of this fruit will live forever, for the curse of sin has been broken. Ironically enough, it was at Golgotha, the place of the skull, that David buried the giant Goliath's head. Centuries later, on this same plot of ground, Jesus' cross was erected. When it penetrated Golgotha, it crushed the skull, just as God promised several thousand years prior in the Garden. At long last, the masterplan had come together. It was finished!

XVI: IT'S A TRAP

Date: c. AD 30
Location: Bethany, Judea

"Take away the stone!"

Martha of Bethany stared speechless at Jesus, along with her friends and Jesus' disciples. Had she heard Jesus wrong? "But, Lord," she said in a patient voice, so as not to seem disobedient and doubtful of the rabbi's claim, "by this time there is a bad odor, for he has been in there for four days."

Mary, like all Jews, was familiar with the popular superstition that the human soul could return to the body on the third day and resuscitate the once deceased human being. However, in the case of Martha's brother, Lazarus, he had been dead for four days, one day past the possibility of superstition. Yet, the place where men deem a situation too far gone is where God likes best to show His power.

Jesus could hear the murmur of the crowds around Him. The doubtful thoughts of His disciples echoed in His ears, but Jesus was undaunted by the crowd's unbelief. Thousands of

244 | The Way Up Came Down

men and women had openly voiced their criticism and utter rejection of Jesus' words before, but never once did Jesus pander to the crowd. Never once did He cave into peer pressure, but rather, grounded in the truth, Jesus preached the unimaginable, that all things were possible with God.

Turning to Martha, Jesus said, "Did I not tell you that if you believe, you will see the glory of God?"

Martha instantly recalled Jesus' words moments prior when she first received news that Jesus was approaching the village. Both Martha and her sister Mary had sent messengers days before to Jesus concerning their brother's serious illness. As good friends of Jesus, they had hoped that the famous miracle worker would show mercy upon their household and heal their brother Lazarus.

Day after day passed and still no word. Then Lazarus died. The two sisters had held onto hope, telling their brother that they had sent word to Jesus, believing that He would not forsake them in their hour of need. They had consistently housed Him, fed Him, and taken care of His twelve apostles. Surely, the least Jesus could do was heal His own friend. He had healed strangers. No doubt He would come running once He heard His friend was near death.

Such was not the case. Lazarus died. Mary and Martha buried him, convinced they had seen the last of their brother. The days when the sound of his laughter had filled their house, when he had settled disputes between his two sisters, and when they had hosted his friends, were over.

And then Jesus decided to show up. Convenient. No sooner did Martha learn of His arrival did she take off running to meet Him. While before she would wait for Jesus to come to her door and bustle about with preparations, this time she left the others behind and raced to Him. She did even allow Him to enter the town before demanding an explanation.

Darting to meet Him, Martha vented her pent-up exasperation and frustration. "Lord," she said, "if you had been here, my brother would not have died. But I know that even now God will give you whatever you ask."

Sure, Jesus showed up late, but Martha believed that Jesus never truly showed up late. His very arrival produced hope in her spirit. She did not know what He planned to do next, but she was confident that God was with Him, granting Jesus the power to do anything.

Moved by Martha's profession, Jesus answered her with a solemn word of affirmation. "Your brother will live again."

"I know he will rise again in the resurrection at the last day." Martha's hope began to dwindle as she perceived Jesus' statement to refer to a future, eschatological event. However, Jesus' next surprise shook her to the core.

He said to her, "I am the resurrection and the life. The one who believes in me will live, even though they die; and whoever lives by believing in me will never die. Do you believe this?"

These words were hard for any mortal human being to accept. Martha had heard Jesus teach many profound words of wisdom, but this was nothing short of a claim to divinity. Only God gave life. Who did Jesus think He was?

Her hands clasped together, Martha bowed her head in humble subservience. "Yes, Lord," she replied, "I believe that you are the Messiah, the Son of God, who is to come into the world" (John 11:27).

Remembering these words as Jesus commanded the men to move the stone, Martha felt convicted in her spirit. After a deep breath, she exhaled and prepared herself for the inevitable. She then joined her sister Mary, and the two watched intently as several men stepped forward and rolled away the stone.

Instantly, Martha could distinguish the decaying smell. Death had begun its destruction. At this point, Martha nearly lost all hope, having witnessed firsthand the power and cruelty of death. But, turning her gaze toward Jesus, she now fixed her eyes on Him whom she had come to respect and trust. In fact, all eyes were set on Jesus as He boldly approached the open grave with palpable confidence. With each step Jesus took closer to the grave, Martha felt her anticipation soar to new heights. Something miraculous was about to happen!

At last, Jesus came to a stop several paces from the tomb so that He could clearly perceive Lazarus' body wrapped in linen. Flies circled his body, inflicting further humiliation on Martha's already deceased brother. Nonetheless, Jesus' eyes projected a determination that could not be thwarted even by a force as powerful as death itself.

Death was a punishment inflicted by the power of the Almighty Creator, thus, a power equal to the One who enacted the punishment was required to break the bonds of death. For Jesus to raise Lazarus, He had to have the power of God Himself.

Behind Jesus, a vast crowd of men, women, and children gathered to see what would take place next. Religious leaders mocked Jesus under their breath, commoners watched in anticipation, and the sisters of Lazarus prayed earnestly that the power of God might be exhibited in and through Jesus.

Sensing the weight of the moment, Jesus refused to fall into the sin of pride and bathe in the spotlight. Rather, He wanted to ensure that all glory was given to the One who deserved it, the very one who sent Him into the world to bring dead people like Lazarus back to life.

All eyes on Him, Jesus lifted His head to the heavens, a smile on His face, and prayed in a loud voice so that all might hear Him. "Father, I thank you that you have heard me. I knew that you always hear me, but I said this for the benefit of the people standing here, that they may believe that you sent me."

Lowering His gaze, Jesus narrowed His eyes together. With a thunderous command, He bellowed, "Lazarus, come out!"

All of a sudden, the corpse that was once Lazarus began to move.

Horrified, the Jewish religious leaders backed away in trepidation. "He's possessed by demons!" some hissed.

A tear trickled down Jesus' face as Lazarus began to peel away his linen, yet upon locking eyes with Jesus, Lazarus ceased his efforts and immediately approached his healer. Unable to hold back the wave of tears welled up inside him, Lazarus wept before the feet of Jesus.

Taking compassion on His friend, Jesus commanded for those present to help Lazarus out of his grave clothes.

Martha instantly rushed to her brother's side, kissing and embracing him. As she helped her brother out of his linen clothes, however, she could not help but look back over her shoulder as Jesus returned to His apostles.

All Martha's theology collapsed in on itself as she reflected on Jesus' words to her. "I am the resurrection."

At first, Martha did not know what Jesus meant by this statement, but now she had living proof of Jesus' claim. Resurrection was not an intellectual construct. Rather, it was a present reality incarnated in Jesus, the Living God! Truly, He was resurrection, and all life held its balance in Him.

Less than a year later, Jesus' corpse lies as motionless as Lazarus did on that fateful day not too long ago. He who claimed to be the resurrection and the life was dead. Even so, while others could not perceive it, the raising of Lazarus was a dress rehearsal for the greater resurrection to come. The Resurrecting King was not yet finished resurrecting.

Incognito Disciples

Upon Jesus' crucifixion, the Bible says that "Joseph of Arimathea asked Pilate for the body of Jesus" (John 19:38). Joseph, a member of the Jewish Sanhedrin (the ruling council), had been a disciple of Jesus, but not openly for fear of the other Jewish leaders (John 19:28). For Joseph to have followed Jesus openly, he would have incurred political, social, and financial reparations.

In truth, Jesus has many disciples today who, out of fear of the reprisal of others, choose to follow Him in secret. Courage does not visit a man overnight, and it is better to follow God in secret than not to follow Him at all (Daniel 6:10). Eventually, though, even private followers must come out into the light. Jesus Himself cautioned that if we denied Him, He would deny us. He also warned us that it would cost us to follow Him, but the gains are out of this world! So Joseph took the gamble.

The Sanhedrin had recently condemned Jesus to death. Accordingly, all those associated with Him were likely to be punished on His account. Joseph was risking both his standing in the Sanhedrin and in Jewish society, but he deemed the risk worth it. Because of his love for Jesus, he risked becoming an outcast. He had failed successfully to beg for Jesus' life, and so now, he must beg for Christ's corpse.

Thus, it was yet another humiliation of Jesus that His body, unclaimed by His own disciples, was handed over to a member of the very group that condemned Him. Yet since His body remained unclaimed by His closest disciples, Joseph spared Christ a far worse humiliation. By requesting His body for burial, he prevented Christ's body from being unceremoniously cast into a pit with the bodies of the two thieves.

Joseph could not simply take Jesus down from the cross and claim Him for himself. Rather, Joseph had to seek permission from the Roman magistrate to do so. God could have had angels bury His Son, or even done so Himself as He had done for Moses, but instead, Christ had Joseph, a mortal man, beg for Jesus' body from the very one who ordered Jesus' execution.

Surprised at Jesus' early death, Pilate conceded to Joseph's request and delivered Jesus' body over to him. Thus, with the help of Nicodemus, Joseph removed Jesus' corpse from Cavalry's cruel cross.

This Nicodemus was the same individual who previously met with Christ in search of answers regarding the kingdom of Heaven (John 3). Like Joseph, he approached Christ in secret. He had great respect for Jesus and His teachings, but he was not willing to publicly associate himself with Christ's followers. Thus, both he and Joseph abstained from casting a vote during Jesus' trial, unwilling to vote in favor of Jesus' crucifixion but equally unwilling to vote in favor of sparing His life (Mark 14:64).

Even so, when the time of Christ's death arrived and His apostles were nowhere to be found, these two men stepped forward, discontent to hide in the shadows anymore. Most people in their shoes would have seen the death of Christ as a sign to distance themselves further from Him. Both Joseph and Nicodemus acted otherwise. Jesus' death, which shocked His public disciples, gave courage to His secret disciples.

Perhaps it was out of shame that Joseph and Nicodemus tended to Jesus' body. Maybe it was with tears that these two men wept over Jesus' corpse, mourning over the loss of a rabbi they held near and dear to their hearts.

Regardless of what emotions forced these men into the light, from this point forward they were willing to associate themselves with the name of Jesus. While others fled, they stepped openly into the light, knowing full well the trials that awaited them on account of their faith. Their love for Jesus surpassed their fears of their enemies, and so it should be for all those who follow Christ.

Joseph of Arimathea, a man declared to be both good and righteous, was in search of the kingdom of God all his life, but his search ceased when he beheld the corpse of Christ. While the rest of the Sanhedrin believed Christ to be a blasphemer, Joseph knew that in the very bones and blood of Christ lay the kingdom of God incarnate (Luke 23:51). Thus, any disservice he faced at the hands of his accusers he considered minuscule in comparison to the surpassing worth of Christ and His kingdom.

The Burial of Jesus

In preparation for Jesus' burial, Nicodemus provided "a mixture of myrrh and aloes, about seventy-five pounds" (John 19:39). The amount of spices Nicodemus brought was equivalent to that used to bury a king, which was indeed fitting for the burial of Jesus. According to sacrifices, God would often declare the sacrifice to be a sweet-smelling aroma. Thus, Jesus' death and burial were quite literally and spiritually a pleasing aroma to the nostrils of God.

Despite his previous skepticism, Nicodemus had come to accept that Jesus was not a lunatic. Nor was He a liar. Rather, He was a great king and worthy of a correspondingly suitable burial.

Giving no thought to expense, Nicodemus ensured that Jesus's body was treated with utmost dignity. He was mistreated in life, but Nicodemus would ensure He was well attended in death.

Nicodemus and Joseph proceeded to wrap Jesus' body in strips of linen after dousing Jesus' body with spices. In this way, Jesus' grave clothes became our wedding garments. He allowed Himself to be wrapped in the garbs of the dead, so that we might be clothed with the raiments of the living.

The Garden

Following Jesus' preparation for burial, Joseph and Nicodemus proceeded to transport Jesus' corpse to the place of burial.

According to the Gospel of John, "At the place where Jesus was crucified, there was a garden, and in the garden a new tomb, in which no one had ever been laid" (John 19:39).

In Genesis 2, God placed the first two human beings, Adam and Eve in the Garden of Eden. There, in the Garden, Adam and Eve fell into sin and ushered in the penalty of death.

Centuries later, Christ would begin and end His passion week in a Garden. He would face betrayal and abandonment in the Garden of Gethsemane, and ultimate victory in the Garden near Golgotha. Thus, in a Garden humanity fell, and in a Garden, humanity was redeemed.

The Holy Sepulcher

Joseph's tomb, in which he placed Jesus, was a burial place cut into solid rock. Even in death, Jesus suffered humiliation. He was born in a manger, with no room in the inn, and now He would be buried in another man's tomb.

Thankfully for Joseph and Nicodemus, the tomb was said to not be too far from the place of Jesus' execution. In other words, the tomb was in close proximity to the cross.

This is the same for the Christian faith. The cross of Cavalry and the Holy Sepulcher are closely related. Without one, the other would be meaningless. Without Jesus' death, His resurrection would never have occurred. Yet, without His resurrection, His death would have been in vain. Both are intimately linked and essential to the hope and convictions of all believers.

Because of the tomb's relatively close vicinity, Joseph and Nicodemus laid Jesus' body to rest there, so as not to disrupt the Jewish Day of Preparation. The Day of Preparation involved undertaking the necessary arrangements for the Sabbath that followed after. Thus, with all haste, the two men laid Jesus to rest in the tomb and sealed it.

The tomb itself was significant for one important factor; it had never been used before. It was a virgin tomb, befitting Christ, who was born from a virgin womb. His pure conception required a pure burial. He could not be mixed with the dust of ordinary men, but rather, even in death, He would be set apart.

Not only was He set apart in terms of burial in a virgin tomb, but Christ was also set apart from Jewish society in the fact that He was buried outside of the Holy City. The Jews feared burying the dead amongst the living, believing that the dead would cause ceremonial uncleanliness. But with His resurrection, Christ removed the impurity of death.

Furthermore, Jesus' burial outside the Holy City, Jerusalem, signified His distinction from prevalent Jewish views. Jewish society as a whole centered on the Holy City and the Temple therein. In His death outside the city, Christ displayed His distinct nature from that of human beliefs. No city is holy in and of itself; it is the presence of God that makes things sacred. Thus, to remind the Jews of the proper correlation between holiness and God, Jesus chose to distance Himself from Jerusalem. Both His death and His resurrection would take place outside the city limits, outside the scope of exclusive Jewish practices.

Silent Saturday

For many people, the Saturday in between Christ's burial and His resurrection often goes overlooked. However, each of those three days, Friday through Sunday, signifies something significant in the life of Christ and all believers. Saturday was no exception.

It was no coincidence that the full day Jesus spent in the grave was that of a Saturday, the day of the week God prescribed to rest. In the beginning of Genesis, after God finished creating the world, the Bible says that He rested on the last day, that being Saturday. When God "rested," He illustrated to all His Creation the finality of an illustrious work.

When Christ spent all Saturday in the grave, He signified a similar time of rest. He had done a great work, on par with that of Creation. Thus, He rested.

Many people mistakenly misconstrue God's rest for His absence, but God does not rest like people do. Rather, even in

His rest, He is at work. While Saturday, the day between prom-ise and fulfillment, may seem cold and lonely, God is at work. It may feel like He is asleep, leaving us alone and afraid, but even in our moments of seeming loneliness, God is at work. If you listen closely, you will not hear silence, but rather you will hear the word of God remind you that Sunday is coming. The day of reckoning is near. Behold, the day of the Lord approaches!

The Guard at the Tomb

Shortly after Jesus' burial, on the day following Preparation Day, the chief priests and Pharisees petitioned Pilate concern-ing Jesus' body.

> "Sir," they said, "we remember that while he was still alive that deceiver said, 'After three days I will rise again.' So give the order for the tomb to be made secure until the third day. Otherwise, his disciples may come and steal the body and tell the people that he has been raised from the dead. This last deception will be worse than the first."
>
> Matthew 27:63-64

Notice how while Jesus' own disciples doubted the clar-ity and possibility of Jesus' resurrection, Jesus' enemies, the ones responsible for His death, had no such ambiguity in their minds. They knew exactly what Jesus meant when He referred to the sign of Jonah (Matt. 12:38-41).

One day, when the Pharisees pressed Jesus for a sign, He rebuked them saying He would give them no sign but the sign of Jonah. "For as Jonah was three days and three nights in the belly of a huge fish, so the Son of Man will be three days and three nights in the heart of the earth" (Matt. 12:40). The Jewish religious leaders knew that simply because Jesus' body was stuffed away in a tomb did not mean that the story of this Nazarene was over. If they could secure the tomb until the third day, however, they would succeed in quelling this narrative. By appealing to Pilate, instead of using their own guards, the chief priests and Pharisees attempted to make a statement: that anyone who violated the tomb would forfeit their lives.

Unbeknownst to them, they had very little to fear from Jesus' disciples. All of them, save John, abandoned Him completely. They remained cowering in fear in the upper room, too afraid to venture outside lest they face a similar fate to that of their Master.

Even so, Pilate grants the request of the Jewish leaders and provides both guards and a seal. The guards were present to thwart any attempt at opening the grave, while the seal, imprinted on ropes, was present to deter any future threats after the guards should leave. Breaking a Roman seal was punishable by death, and thus, very few would be willing to risk raiding Jesus' tomb.

Setting up camp outside Jesus' tomb, the Roman soldiers mocked the corpse inside, scoffing at the idea of guarding a dead man in His tomb. Yet, despite the best efforts of the Roman and Jewish authorities, Jerome, an early church father, notes that, "The greater their precautionary care, the more fully is revealed the power of the resurrection" (Commentary on Matthew, 4.27.64). The soldiers thought that this act of service was the easiest in their career, yet they would find that keeping a dead man in His grave was far more difficult than they could ever have expected.

Conclusion

In the blockbuster film *Star Wars: Return of the Jedi* the Imperial forces managed to lure the Rebel Alliance into a trap by leading them to believe that the Death Star, the Empire's super weapon, was vulnerable. Seizing the bait, the rebels attacked the Death Star, only to find they had played right into the Empire's hands. Shocked, the rebel admiral famously yelled out, "It's a trap!"

Just as the Imperials orchestrated an ambush for the unsuspecting Rebel Alliance, so God Himself devised a snare for sin and death. When Jesus died, death was certain it had emerged victorious. The trap death intended for Jesus, however, was actually designed by God Himself. The moment death thought it had snared Jesus, Jesus opened His eyes and winked. "Gotcha!"

Just as the Red Sea was the means of salvation to God's people and destruction to their enemies, so the cross of Christ is salvation to all those who believe and devastation to His enemies. It's a set up! The crucifixion was a set up from the beginning, formulated by God to act as the means by which mankind could be returned to an intimate relationship with Him. Yet, for the crucifixion to have meaning, there needed to be resurrection.

XVII: ROLLING STONES

Date: c. 586-538 BC
Location: Unspecified Valley

Ezekiel's eyes scanned the dusty, desert valley. It was cold, but there was no wind in the midst of the valley, and all about Ezekiel, as far as his eyes could see, were discombobulated bones. The bones of hundreds of warriors littered the surrounding premises, victims of a fierce battle that failed to end in their favor.

Ezekiel immediately identified the fallen soldiers as the people of Israel, whom King Nebuchadnezzar of Babylon had scattered and dispersed across the known world. In the hopeless situation, many Jews, such as Ezekiel, doubted whether or not the Jewish people would come together once again. In the midst of doubt and anxiety, however, the Word of God consulted Ezekiel.

"Son of Man, can these bones live?"

God most commonly referred to Ezekiel as "Son of Man" as a reminder of his finite nature and the eternal power of God. Thus, as Ezekiel looked about, he realized that no power inherent in man could ever accomplish such a feat. No man could gather the Jewish people again, let alone raise a valley of dry bones to life. Yet, in answer to God's question, Ezekiel said, "Sovereign Lord, you alone know."

Only God knows. Man can speculate what God has determined. In the end, though, only God knows what the future holds, only He knows what is possible.

Upon Ezekiel's response, God commanded Ezekiel:

> Prophesy to these bones and say to them, "Dry bones, hear the word of the Lord! This is what the Sovereign Lord says to these bones: I will make breath enter you, and you will come to life. I will attach tendons to you and make flesh come upon you and cover you with skin; I will put breath in you, and you will come to life. Then you will know that I am the Lord."
>
> Ezekiel 37:4-6

Who could give breath to the bones? Who could grant life? Not Ezekiel, but God Himself. Resurrection is not granted for men to wield; it is the sole power of God to wield it at His discretion.

Obediently, Ezekiel began to prophesy to the dry bones. His actions did not make sense in his mind but allowing his belief to take rest in his heart, Ezekiel forsook all logical thinking and began to prophesy. As he did so, "[T]here was a noise, a rattling sound, and the bones came together, bone to bone."

Ezekiel could hear the rattle all around him, echoing in the desert valley, as the disoriented bones began to draw together. It was an incredible sight, one Ezekiel could not fully grasp, but resurrection is not something meant to be understood. It is something meant to be accepted!

As the bones drew together, "[T]endons and flesh appeared on them and skin covered them, but there was no breath in them."

The valley, formerly composed of bones, was replaced by a field of corpses. Despite Ezekiel's prophesying, the bones could not come together by his word. Rather, the ability to restore life is possessed by God alone. Ezekiel was as helpless to bring life to the corpses as Elisha was to raise the Shunammite woman's son. In Ezekiel's moment of weakness, however, God poured forth His strength.

Addressing Ezekiel, God said, "Prophesy to the breath; prophesy, son of man, and say to it, 'This is what the Sovereign Lord says: Come, breath, from the four winds and breathe into these slain, that they may live.'"

Ezekiel remembered well how Adam, in the Garden of Eden, received the breath of God and was brought to life. The connection between the Spirit of God and life was unmistakable, for the Spirit gives life and is life.

Thus, once again, Ezekiel followed God's command, and as he did so, "breath entered [the dry bones]; they came to life and stood up on their feet — a vast army" (Ez. 27:10).

The dry bones had been dead for a while. They had been sitting in their graves for quite some time, but God said to Ezekiel, concerning the bones and the people of Israel, "My people, I am going to open your graves and bring you up from them."

God is the Resurrecting King. Whether it is dry bones in a desert or a tombstone in a garden, when God says move, all— dead or alive—will move!

The plain symbolized a place of seeming defeat, but what Israel's enemies deemed as defeat, God proved to be a point of resurrection. In the same way, everyone, Jesus friends and His enemies, perceived His death to be a sign of defeat. Yet, it was this seemingly hopeless situation that bore the fruit of resurrection.

God transforms bones into armies, graves into gardens, and death into life. Like Ezekiel centuries before, the Roman soldiers had felt a trembling and heard a terrifying sound that made them tremble in trepidation. It was the rattling sound of the resurrection. [7]

The rattle of Earth and the Word of Heaven intermingled as the universe cried out as one for the Creator to rise up once more and take His place among the living.

The Earthquake

The hours wore on, and Saturday passed. Sunday dawned, and nothing happened. The Roman soldiers began to shake their heads in disbelief. Caiaphas and his band of cronies put too much stock in the words of a dead man. Jesus' disciples were nowhere to be found and made no such attempts to steal Jesus' body. Jesus was still very much dead.

Undoubtedly, they thought that Jesus' body would begin to decay, and worms and maggots would eat His flesh. The herbs with which Nicodemus doused Jesus' body would soon wear off, replaced by the foul odor that plagued all dead men.

Just when the soldiers prepared to call it quits, thinking their job was done, just when it seemed like Jesus' word would never come to fruition, "there was a great earthquake" (Matt. 28:2).

The moment Jesus died, the earth shook out of agony (Matt. 27:51), but upon the announcement of His resurrection, the earth leapt for joy. Unable to contain its excitement, the earth prophesied in ways beyond that of human speech.

The created gave praise to the Creator, as He said it would (Luke 19:40).

The rattle of resurrection echoed in the tomb of Christ as dead bones came alive again. The Lord Jesus was not dead. Behold, He was only "asleep," and the effects of this earthquake would tremor forever after, unto the end of the earth.

The Officer of Heaven

Upon the signal of the earthquake, "an angel of the Lord came down from Heaven" (Matt. 28:2). Throughout Jesus' earthly ministry, angels often tended to Him. They were present at His birth, after His temptation, and in the Garden of Gethsemane right before His arrest. We find no mention of their presence following His arrest and preceding His resurrection. Without a doubt, Jesus Himself affirmed that He could have requested His Father send a legion of angels to rescue Him, but Jesus gave no such order. Rather, He endured the cross alone. The angels forsook Him, His own Father turned away from Him, but Jesus persevered.

Thus, upon the dawn of His resurrection, the angels returned to the One who reclaimed the glory He had prior to the creation of the world. With great joy, an angel came down from Heaven and "going to the tomb, rolled back the stone" (Matt. 28:2).

In His resurrected form, Jesus later showed His apostles His ability to pass through solid objects, thus proving the stone an inadequate object to restrain His glory. Accordingly, the angel moved the stone not so Jesus could come out, but so others could go in.

Jesus could have moved the stone Himself, but He allowed the angel to do it. If Jesus moved the stone in His own power, it would have symbolized a jailbreak. It would seem that Jesus was violating His sentence, instead of submitting to it.

The same action by an angel, on the other hand, signified the will of Heaven. The Father had judged Jesus innocent, and so, the bailiff of Heaven was sent to set Him free.

Following his removing the stone, the angel sat on the stone, as if daring the Roman soldiers to push the stone back into place. Not even all the powers of Hell and death could undo what Jesus had just done. The stone that required all God's enemies to seal was removed by the mere command of God.

Pilate had sent his soldiers to secure the tomb, but a single officer from Jesus' army was sufficient to strike terror into the battle-hardened Romans. "The guards were so afraid of him that they shook and became like dead men" (Matt. 28:4). Never before had they witnessed such an awful sight.

Yet, moments later, when several women would venture near the now empty tomb, the angel would command them, "Do not be afraid" (Matt. 28:5). The resurrection, which brings fear to the enemies of the cross, brings joy to those who believe in Christ.

The New Creation

In Jewish culture, as previously mentioned, Jews honored the Sabbath day (Saturday). In commemoration of the day on which God rested from His work, Jews laid aside all work and followed God's example. In the case of Jesus, after resting all day Saturday, He rose Sunday morning, on the first day, to begin a new work.

On Easter Sunday, Jesus ushered in a new world, a new creation, one where humanity was finally restored to God through the shed blood of Jesus Christ and resurrection of His body. Thus, Christians around the world celebrate this holy day, that of Sunday, in remembrance of the work of Christ that He accomplished that one fateful Sunday.

In the very beginning of Creation, the first thing God created, on what would later be called Sunday, was light. It is no irony at all that Jesus Himself claimed to be the Light of the World (John 18:12). On Easter Sunday, the light shone into the darkness, and the darkness could not overcome it (John 1:5). The light of Heaven extinguished the darkness of the grave as the Father commanded once more, "Let there be light!"

And behold, there was light! The first day of the new creation.

Rabboni!

Bitter tears trickled down Mary's face as she wept soberly over her master's fate. To some, Jesus of Nazareth was a good teacher, to others, He was a raving lunatic, but to Mary, He was both a friend and a healer.

Later legends would villainize Mary of Magdala as a prostitute or even portray her as the wife of Christ, but such were unsubstantiated, propagated lies. Mary was nothing out of the ordinary. Just another lowly individual the Almighty God showed His favor upon.

Mary's tears dotted the ground as she bowed her head in reverence before the tomb of Jesus. Even now, she could still sense the aura of power emanating from the place He had once been kept. His body was missing, but she could still feel His presence.

She remembered well the first time she encountered Him, His eyes penetrating to Mary's very soul. At that point in time, Mary was possessed by seven demons, foul spirits who tortured her day in and day out. Yet, when Jesus walked in the room, fear had to flee. With power that even the exorcists did not have, Jesus cast the spirits out of Mary and restored her to a life far greater than her previous one. Mary knew from that day forth that there was no going back. With Jesus at her side, no evil spirit of the abyss could ever chain her again.

However, demon possession was not the only obstacle Mary had to overcome in her life. Unfortunately, the Jewish culture of her day was not well-known for its treatment of women. Women were deemed lesser than men, and the more "spiritual" men would often pray thanking God that they were neither a Gentile, nor a woman, in that order. However, Jesus showed compassion on women and had a number of them follow Him from town to town.

One of the closest females to Jesus, Mary was present at many of His miracles, and even at the cross. While the other disciples forsook Jesus in His last hour, Mary and Jesus' female followers remained with Him to the bitter end. Jesus had helped Mary in her greatest hour of pain, and so, the least she could do was remain with Him in His moment of trial.

Scarring images warped Mary's mind as she recalled the brutal flogging and crucifixion of her Lord. Yet, through it all, Jesus never once offered resistance. She had seen Him raise the dead and experienced Him cast out spirits, but this time was different. This time, maintaining astounding self-control in the face of false accusations, Jesus did nothing. It was not like Him.

Usually, He was a man of action. But when His own life was at risk, He did not even defend Himself.

Yet, unbeknownst to Mary, it was not any nail that kept Jesus to the cross on Golgotha. It was His self-control. It was His obedience. And it was us. Scripture says, "For the joy set before Him, he endured the cross" (Heb. 12:2). The pleasure of His Father and an eternal relationship with us awaited Him. Rather than doing "nothing," Jesus was doing exactly what was necessary to complete the Father's plan to redeem mankind. Mary, though, did not yet understand this.

All she understood was that her beloved Lord was dead and now His body was missing. Entering the tomb, Mary perceived the two angels she had previously seen with the other women when they first arrived at the tomb. The angels, seeing Mary's depressed countenance, asked, "Woman, why are you weeping?"

Blubbering through tears, Mary answered, "They have taken away my Lord, and I do not know where they have laid him."

Despite the angelic presence, Mary still doubted the words the angels spoke to her concerning Jesus' resurrection. They clearly told her and the other women that God raised Jesus from the dead, but Mary did not believe. She needed to see the proof!

Turning around, she was caught by surprise when she saw who she thought to be the gardener coming towards her.

The man, seeing Mary's tears, asked, "Woman, why are you weeping? Whom are you seeking?"

This was the second time Mary had been asked this question. The first, by the angels, and now, by this man. Thinking this man to be the gardener, Mary begged, "Sir, if you have carried him away, tell me where you have laid him, and I will take him away."

Mary did not want to see the body of her Lord desecrated. So convinced was she that Jesus was dead, that she asked to see the corpse. She heard Jesus formerly prophesy concerning His future resurrection, but when the time came, she doubted. Even so, she showed honor to her Lord in her request. Not wanting to see Jesus' body ill-treated, she begged to be given possession of Him. If religious men of power like Joseph of Arimathea could not provide Jesus the decency He was due, then a formerly possessed woman would.

Addressing the woman, the man called her by name. "Mary!"

Mary choked mid-tears and gasped in awe. Her hands clasped over her mouth, she looked at the man with open eyes. *"Rabboni!"*

Standing before Mary in resurrected form was none other than the Lord Jesus. He whom she came to see in the tomb was alive once more.

Why Mary?

So, why Mary? Of all the people Jesus could have revealed Himself to first on the day of His resurrection, why did He choose to show up to this woman? Mary was no one significant. True, she was one of Jesus' donors and a close companion, but what influence did she have?

If I had risen from the grave (a huge hypothetical), I would have chosen differently. Maybe, I would have appeared to Tiberius Caesar, the sovereign of the Roman Empire. By appearing to Caesar, Jesus could have instantly infiltrated the center of the known world and perhaps brought about immediate revival. Or what if Jesus appeared to Pilate? Pilate was the very one who condemned Him to death. By showing up to Pilate, Jesus would have possibly found a convert of greater proportion than the Apostle Paul.

The list could go on and on of potential candidates Jesus could have revealed Himself to after His resurrection for advantageous purposes, but the fact remains that the omniscient God chose to appear to Mary. In this manner, Jesus revealed that the Gospel is meant for ordinary, seemingly insignificant people like Mary, not just for the rich and powerful. Just like His birth was announced to lowly shepherds and rich, wise men alike, so His resurrection is available to all. While the rich and powerful—the Roman soldiers and the chief priests—rejected the resurrection, the destitute and hopeless joyously accepted the salvation extended to them.

Additionally, Mary sought out Jesus. She went to the tomb looking for Him. God promises that if you seek Him, you will find Him. That is exactly what happened to Mary, who is an example for all of us.

Moreover, Mary was able to face Sunday because she was there on Friday. She experienced resurrection as a product of her acceptance of death. This way, Mary's testimony illustrates that if we want to see resurrection in our own lives, we must first be willing to accept death. We must first be willing to approach the cross. Unless we kneel at the cross, we cannot honestly appreciate the empty tomb.

Accept Death

For many of us, this is difficult because we do not want to accept death. We want to press on, for God to make our lives better—to make us more moralistic, more loving, more this and more that. As G. K. Chesterton observed, though, "Jesus does not offer to make bad people good but to make dead people alive!" God's Word puts it this way: "But because of his great love for us, God, who is rich in mercy, *made us alive with Christ even when we were dead in transgressions*" (Eph. 2:4-5) (emphasis added). The truth is that many atheists today live "good," moralistic lives, but their deeds are not credited to them for they were never alive to begin with. Following Jesus should cause us to lead better lives, but not to earn salvation, rather because we have passed from death to life. We are dead to sin and alive to Christ, and, accordingly, the love of Christ compels us to live for Him and not for ourselves.

Salvation is not a testimony of how we came to God, rather it is a testimony of how God came to us and how we answered His call! "But God demonstrates his own love for us in this: While we were still sinners, Christ died for us" (Rom. 5:8). We were powerless, unable to earn God's favor, and yet He rescued us. "For it is by grace you have been saved, through faith – and this is not from yourselves, it is the gift of God – not by works, so that no one can boast" (Eph. 2:8-9). Thus, for us to experience the power of Jesus' resurrection, we must first experience the tragedy of death. When I die to self, I acknowledge that "I have been crucified with Christ and I no longer live, but Christ lives in me. The life I now live in the body, I live by faith in the Son of God, who loved me and gave himself for me" (Gal. 2:20). Once we take the step of faith and surrender our lives, that is when we truly live.

Deny Self

The choice to die is also the choice to live. To die to ourselves, we must deny ourselves, take up our cross daily, and follow Jesus (Luke 9:23). To deny someone means to refuse to have companionship with them any longer, to be separated from them. To deny yourself is to totally distance yourself from the person you were, to say, "I don't know the man!"

In one of the scenes from NBC's sitcom *The Office*, one of the characters named Ryan reveals that in the past he had knocked the mirror off someone else's car in the office parking lot. Realizing that it had been his car, Kevin confronts Ryan.

Kevin: "You knocked the mirror off of my car?"

Ryan: "Yeah, isn't that messed up?"

Kevin: "Yeah."

Ryan: "That guy did a lot of things I'm not proud of."

Kevin: "Wait, when you say 'that guy,' do you mean you?"

Ryan: "I mean the guy I *used* to be. I'm Ryan 2.0. And, if it makes you feel any better, that guy did a lot of messed up stuff to me, too."

While Ryan attempts to distance himself from his former ways to deflect responsibility, he unwittingly illustrates for many of us what it means to deny oneself. It means that we are no longer who we used to be; we are new creatures. "[I]f anyone is in Christ, he is a new creation. The old has passed away; behold, the new has come" (2 Cor. 5:17). The Greek meaning for "new creation" refers to a creation that has never before been seen on Earth. Since we are new creations, sin has no hold on us, for we no longer possess the sin nature attributed by Adam. We have become slaves to righteousness, not slaves to sin. We become this new creature, a product of the resurrection, at the moment of salvation. We continue this process of transformation as we deny ourselves, take up our cross, and follow Jesus daily.

In the end, we are left with the paradox Jesus posed to His disciples: "[W]hoever wants to save their life will lose it, but whoever loses their life for me and for the gospel will save it" (Mark 8:35). The choice is ours. Which will you choose?

Conclusion

In my younger days, I often wondered why Christians called the day of Jesus' crucifixion "Good Friday." Why was it good that Jesus was barbarically killed? God revealed to me that the reason Friday was good was because Easter Sunday was coming. Believers call Friday "good" because we have the benefit of hindsight. Were it not for Easter Sunday, however, Good Friday would just be 'Friday.'

The crux of the Christian faith, the bedrock of our salvation, rests on the finished work of the resurrection. In his letter to the church at Corinth, Paul would later write concerning the death and resurrection of Christ that if "Christ has not been raised, our preaching is useless and so is your faith...And if Christ has not been raised, your faith is futile; you are still in your sins" (1 Cor. 15:14, 17). Had Jesus died for our sins and not been raised, either He would be a liar for not keeping His word or He would deny us the prospect of a bodily resurrection. Yet, the Scriptures foretell a day when believers shall receive a glorified body, a body which can be received only because death has been conquered.

Significantly, one should note just how unnatural death is. Death was not something God initially intended for humanity. Proof of this exists in that virtually every human being shudders at the imminence of death. Indeed, God has set eternity in the human heart (Eccl. 3:11). C.S. Lewis explained it this way in *Mere Christianity*:

> Creatures are not born with desires unless satisfaction for those desires exists. A baby feels hunger: well, there is such a thing as food. A duckling wants to swim: well, there is such a thing as water. Men feel sexual desire: well, there is such a thing as sex. If I find in myself a desire which no experience in this world can satisfy, the most probable explanation is that I was made for another world.

God does not play with our feelings or place a desire in us that He Himself will not fill. Rather, Jesus' death and resurrection paves the way for all those who have faith in His Name to enter into the Kingdom of Heaven as co-heirs of Jesus. No longer do Heaven and Earth exist as two kingdoms divided by a chasm between them, but rather Jesus bridged the chasm for the salvation of the human race. "For Christ also suffered once for sins, the righteous for the unrighteous, to bring you to God" (1 Peter 3:18).

In the words of the Apostle Paul, "'Death has been swallowed up in victory.' 'Where, O death, is your victory? Where, O death, is your sting?' The sting of death is sin, and the power of sin is the law. But thanks be to God! He gives us the victory through our Lord Jesus Christ" (1 Cor. 15:54-57). Thanks be to God that the way up came down!

EPILOGUE

I find it appropriate at this point to meditate on the words of the Apostle John. While exiled on the island of Patmos, John received a vision from God in which he was shown many things. Chief among all these eschatological events and descriptions was that concerning Heaven.

In Revelation 21, John offers the reader a beautiful picture of how God will renew all Creation after His ultimate victory over Satan. John declared that he observed "a new heaven and a new earth, for the first heaven and the first earth had passed away, and there was no longer any sea. I saw the Holy City, the new Jerusalem, coming down out of heaven from God, prepared as a bride beautifully dressed for her husband" (Rev. 21:1-2).

Just as the Bible began with God creating, so the Bible ends with God creating. God is first and foremost a Creator. He is the Author of life, and from the moment He brought the universe into existence, He has never stopped creating. Thus, with the end of sin, Satan, and death, God will create a new cosmos free of the effects of the former created order.

John goes on to declare that he heard a voice like thunder emanating from God's throne saying,

> Look! God's dwelling place is now among the people, and He will dwell with them. They will be his people, and God himself will be with them and be their God. He will wipe every tear from their eyes. There will be no more death or mourning or crying or pain, for the old order of things has passed away.
>
> Revelation 21:3-4

The days of mankind's dwelling in a Garden with only the occasional visitation of God are long gone. For all eternity, those who belong to Christ will forever dwell with Him in Paradise, and He with them. In this manner, the chosen people of God are made manifest. God's chosen people are not simply one nation or tribe, but rather all peoples and nations that come to Him for their renewal.

To these people, God promises they shall never again see death, nor shall they ever experience travesties that might lead to pain or tears. "They will run and not grow weary, they will walk and not be faint" (Is. 40:31). All shall be at peace, for we shall be one with our Lord and Savior forever. The night has passed. Behold, there will ever only be morning (Rev. 22:5).

Heaven shall be the gathering place of God's chosen family, all invited to partake in the glorious adventure of a lifetime. An individual's life on Earth is but a mere precursor to the life to come. The one that shall follow will be unlike anything a mortal being can comprehend.

Human beings, living with angelic creatures and their Holy Creator, will have all eternity to get to know one another and enjoy the Lord's presence. All will be encircled around God's throne with the heavenly choir, singing praises to His majesty. It will be a beautiful concert, all for the praise of One.

Who knows if God will invite people to make their testimonies known, to the glory of God? Perhaps we will be able to hear from, and become acquainted with, the likes of Paul, Peter, David, and Adam, renowned men of the past who each looked forward with longing to this blessed day. Yet, whoever speaks, it shall be that a common thread will tie all their stories together, and that thread is the grace of God, unconditional and undeserving. Every human being in Heaven will enter into the pearly gates only because of this great grace, this truly awesome grace of God.

Thus, I sincerely urge all who read this book to grow in the grace and knowledge of the Lord Jesus Christ. Let His light, the light of Heaven, shine upon you. Ever follow after that light. Press on towards the goal of Heaven, the goal of being One with the Creator. The Day of the Lord draws ever nearer. Oh, beloved of God, may we all look forward to that day with earnest expectancy and each day together declare, "Come, Lord Jesus, come!"

ENDNOTES

Chapter 1

1   One theory theologians suggest is a triune structure of archangels composed of Lucifer, Michael, and Gabriel. Lucifer was considered the archangel of Yahweh, Michael the archangel of the Holy Spirit, and Gabriel the archangel of Jesus. Thus, the heavenly host would be split into three regiments, partially explaining why a third of the angels sided with Lucifer in his rebellion (Rev. 12:4).

Chapter 2

2   Wood, Leon J. The Holy Spirit in the Old Testament, Wipf & Stock Publishers, June 24th, 1998.

Chapter 5

3   A christophany is an appearance of Christ, and these appearances occur throughout the Old and New Testaments. When Jesus met Saul on the road to Damascus, this was a Christophany, and "the Angel of the Lord" is often referenced as a christophany.

Chapter 7

4   In his account of his vision, Jacob (and or the writer Moses) does not describe the physical appearance of God. Perhaps it is because as people, we get so caught up with the physical, and the things we can see, but God shows Jacob and others that He is above our mere physical thoughts. He is above such petty tunnel ways of thinking. Rather, God is an invisible God, who makes Himself known to us in ways we would not have thought possible. He appears to us in more ways than just sight: He visits us in our dreams, He speaks to us in our minds,

He whispers to us in our ears. Yet, while God does not reveal His physical conditions in this passage, He does reveal aspects of His identity.

5   Both Abraham and Isaac only had two sons each. Jacob exceeded them both with twelve sons.

Chapter 13

6   While all religions may superficially appear similar on the outside, they are crucially different on the inside. Specifically, most religions require people to perform certain critical deeds to attain God's approval. Christianity, by contrast, posits that Christ has done everything necessary for people to live in a harmonious relationship with God, both now and forever. In short, most religions are "do" religions, but Christianity is a "done" religion. Thus, the more apt analogy is not that all world religions are different paths leading up the same mountain, but instead that each religion leads up a different mountain, only one of which is home to the true God.

Chapter 17

7   Elevation's 2020 album Graves into Gardens released two singles, "RATTLE!" and "Graves into Gardens," both of which speak to the miracle of the resurrection.

BIBLIOGRAPHY

Avengers: Endgame, Anthony and Joe Russo, 2019. Marvel Studios.

Avengers: Infinity War, Anthony and Joe Russo, 2018. Marvel Studios.

Edwards, Jonathan. *Christ's Agony*. CreateSpace Independent Publishing Platform, April 27, 2017.

ESV Study Bible: English Standard Version. ESV text ed. Wheaton, Ill.: Crossway Bibles, 2008. Moo, Douglas J., Grand Rapids, Mich.: Zondervan Publishing House, 2000.

Furtick, Steven. *Rattle of Resurrection*. Steven Furtick Ministries, April 12, 2020.

Greear, J.D., *A Different Kind of Exclusivity*. J.D. Greear Ministries, April 24, 2019.

Holy Bible, New International Version. Zondervan Publishing House, 1984. (All Scriptural references, unless explicitly stated, are NIV references.)

Keller, Timothy. *The Prodigal Prophet*. London: Hodder & Stoughton, 2018.

Latino, Corazón. *The Truth Behind the Blind Men and the Elephant Analogy*. Anchored in Christ, June 21, 2016.

Lewis, C. S. 1952. *Mere Christianity*. New York: MacMillan Pub. Co.

The Holy Bible: The Amplified Bible. 1987. 2015. La Habra, CA: The Lockman Foundation.

CPSIA information can be obtained
at www.ICGtesting.com
Printed in the USA
LVHW021808141120
671495LV00003B/190

9 781647 734121